# NO!

# NO!

## How One Simple Word
## Can Transform Your Life

## JANA KEMP

AMERICAN MANAGEMENT ASSOCIATION
New York · Atlanta · Brussels · Chicago · Mexico City
San Francisco · Shanghai · Tokyo · Toronto · Washington, D. C.

This publication is designed to provide accurate and authoritative
information in regard to the subject matter covered. It is sold with
the understanding that the publisher is not engaged in rendering
legal, accounting, or other professional service. If legal advice or other
expert assistance is required, the services of a competent professional
person should be sought.

Library of Congress Cataloging-in-Publication Data

Kemp, Jana M.
    No! : how one simple word can transform your life / Jana M. Kemp.
        p.   cm.
    Includes index.
    ISBN 0-8144-7230-3
    1. Assertiveness (Psychology)   I Title: How one simple word can transform your
life.   II. Title.

    BF575.A85K46   2005
    158.2—dc22

                                                                    2004016874

Printing Number

10   9   8   7   6   5   4   3   2   1

# Contents

Preface                                                                                    *vii*

Chapter 1    Introduction: It's Hard to Say *No*                                            1

Chapter 2    The Power of *No*: *No* Is Just as Important as *Yes*                          20

Chapter 3    *No* and Self-Protection: Time, Resources, Self                               38

Chapter 4    The Ethics and Consequences of *No*                                           61

Chapter 5    Saying *No*: You Can Say *No*                                                  80

Chapter 6    Stop Saying *Maybe*: Make a Decision                                          111

Chapter 7    Saying *Yes*                                                                  131

Chapter 8    Decision-Making Practice                                                      143

Chapter 9    More Practice Saying *No*: Final Practice Scenarios                           167

Chapter 10   Keeping Your Resolve                                                          184

Chapter 11   Fifty Mantras for Saying *No*                                                 189

Appendix A   Acknowledgments                                                               197

Appendix B   The Power of No Self-Assessment and Advanced
             Power Practices                                                               201

Appendix C   Long List: Ways to Say *No*                                                   209

Appendix D   Resources and Further Reading                                                 219

Appendix E   Share Your Story: Get a Book                                                  221

*Index*                                                                                    *223*

*About the Author*                                                                         *227*

# *Preface*

We've all done it. Been indecisive when a decision was called for, said *yes* when we meant to say *no*, and found ourselves out of time, out of energy, and out of sorts. It's time to stop being indecisive and start making clear decisions. Why? Because it's not helpful, not respectful, not ethical, and in some cases it is downright dangerous to be indecisive. One of the reasons you act indecisively is that you're not using the word *no* effectively in your daily adult conversations. Until you reclaim the power of *no* in your conversations and in your life, you'll continue being indecisive and be seen as a "Waffler" or a "Yes-ism" person.

*No!* gives you the personal power tool found in the word *no*. In this book you'll learn new ways to ask questions, to think through decisions, to help groups move forward, and to get action to occur. You'll discover ways to:

1. Bring *no* back into your vocabulary without losing friends, family, and jobs (unless it really is time for a change—only you can make that decision).

2. Establish *no* as a power word that protects your time, money, children, health, well-being, and life.

3. Establish the legitimacy of *no* and that not every *no* should be negotiated to a *yes*.

4. Remember phrases and ways of saying *no* whenever you feel *no* is the right thing to say.

Here's what you'll find in the chapters ahead:

Chapter 1: Confirm how hard it is to say no, take the Power of No Self-Assessment, and learn whether your say-no approach is that of a Master of No, Waffler, or Yes-ism person.

Chapter 2: Learn when to say *no* with The Power of No Model™.

Chapter 3: Protect yourself, say *no*. Hear what a *Jeet Kune Do* instructor says about the word *no* and self defense. Learn to use the Decision Priority Grid and to protect yourself, your family, and your assets.

Chapter 4: Understand the ethics and consequences of saying *no*. Are you being ethical when you say *no*, and when you don't say *no*? Learn what an ethics professor says about the word *no* and personal freedom.

Chapter 5: Master saying *no—not ever*. Learn how to say *no*. Learn what your say-no personality is. Discover that you can say *no*.

Chapter 6: Stop waffling, make a decision. Learn how to stop saying phrases such as *no—maybe*. Learn what your waffling-style is. Apply the Power of No Model to put an end to indecision.

Chapter 7: Understand Yes-ism, and that saying "no—not now" is saying "yes later." Practice putting an end to your Yes-ism.

Chapter 8: Practice making daily decisions.

Chapter 9: Practice saying *no*, now while it's safe. Learn from practices that will help you become a Master of No.

Chapter 10: Keep your resolve. Learn strategies to use after having said *no* so that your *no* stays *no*.

Chapter 11: Explore the fifty mantras for saying *no*.

Every chapter has two types of Power Practices. In the first type you are asked to answer questions based on your life experience, so there are not right or wrong answers. The second type of Power Practice is meant for you to test what you are learning and to build your skills for decision making and for saying *no*. Each chapter includes sample potential answers for the Power Practices so that you can determine how well your Yes-ism and waffling behavior is growing into the Master of No skill-set. In the Appendixes, you'll find a second Power of No Self-Assessment along with some advanced power practices, a resource list for learning more about this topic, a long list of words you can use to say *no*, and a page to share your say-no stories.

Throughout the book, I've included quotes from people who responded to e-mailed surveys I used in researching this book. The contributors are cited in Appendix A, and I have their permission to use the material. In some cases their real names are used in the text; in other cases, names were changed.

Here's to your success in mastering one simple word that can transform your life: NO!

# NO!

## CHAPTER 1

# It's Hard to Say No

## POWER PREVIEW POINTS

1. Recognize and accept that saying *no* is difficult.

2. Discover your personal ability to say *no* with the Power of No Self-Assessment.

**D**o you say *no* every time you want to say *no*? This book helps you discover your ability and claim your right to say *no*. And helps you find a balance of personal, professional, and community involvement that inspires you and allows you to complete your commitments without wearing yourself out, short-changing the people important to you, or creating danger for yourself. In other words, now is the time to give yourself permission to say *no*. Now is the time to use the word *no* in daily adult conversations, **not** just conversations with children. No is a powerful word with a time, a place, and thousands of appropriate uses. *No!* is about putting *no* back into your vocabulary as a legitimate, time-saving, and life affirming word. It is about putting an end to indecision and waffling. And finally, this is a book about making a decision and keeping your resolve.

So, when was the last time you said *no*?

"No, thank you, I'm full."
"No, thank you, I'm just looking."
"No, I'm not ready to go yet."

Okay, so you've said *no* several times in the last few days.
What about saying *no* when the stakes are higher and the person

posing the question expects you to say *yes*? In a higher-risk situation like this, when was the last time you said *no*, stuck to it, and felt glad, even relieved because you knew you already had enough to do? If you can't remember the last time you said *no* to anyone or anything, perhaps you too have the *yes*-ism disease. "Yes, I'll help on that project. Yes, I'll be the carpool driver. Yes, I'll answer that call, return that fax, reply to the e-mail, write another memo, schedule another meeting, and *yes*, I'll add that to my to do list so you don't have to." Is it any wonder that by Tuesday of any given week you've depleted your energies and exhausted yourself? Imagine the time you could save by saying *no* even one more time each day.

Besides, do you like saying *yes* so much of the time? Do you look forward to saying *yes* to every question you are asked? Saying *yes* to every invitation you receive or to every request made of you? (See, you can say *no!*)

Remember the 1980s promise that by now we'd all have four-day workweeks with lots of vacation time? And what about the promise that computerization would bring more productivity and less paper consumption? Have you experienced these promised realities? No? Neither have I. And neither has anyone I've met. The last three decades have seen dozens of time-saving, work-reducing, and stress-reducing promises.

And the promises haven't been kept. Our fast-paced, technology driven culture has not reduced stress or workloads. Our time is grabbed at by the very technology that promised to help. Our privacy and our reflective time are diminishing because of technologies that beep, ring, vibrate, speak, and buzz at us. We consume more paper, not less, as promised two decades ago.

Today's stresses and frustrations remind me of last century's phrase, "I'm mad as _____, and I can't take it any more." Today we're shouting, "I'm tired and stressed, isn't there a better way?" Yes. The "better way" is learning to say *no* and mean it, learning to be decisive, and learning to say *yes* only when you mean *yes*.

## POWER PRACTICE: **SAYING YES**

If you find yourself saying *yes* more often than you'd like, here's your chance to uncover the times you say *yes* and would prefer to say *no*.

1. When do you find yourself saying *yes* without thinking about your response?

2. What situations cause you to say *yes* when you'd rather say *no?*

3. Which of your children, coworkers, or friends know how to get you to say *yes* when you mean to say *no?*

4. When have you said *yes* to anything that later put you and your well-being at risk?

5. Whom do you know who is already good at saying *no?* What can you learn from his or her example?

## THE DEFINITION OF *NO*

How do you define the word *no?* The *Miriam Webster's Collegiate Dictionary* shows that the word *no* is used as a noun, as an adjective, and as an adverb. As illustrated by the twelve listed definitions, there are a dozen ways in which the word *no* can be used. In this book, the focus is on the use of the word *no* as a noun. Thus, *no* is "an act or instance of refusing or denying by the use of the word *no*" and is "a negative vote or decision."

The sound-alike words *noh* (a Japanese dance-drama), and *know* (to understand something) are rarely confused with the word *no.* The challenge is that we so rarely hear *no* spoken in daily adult conversations. No tends to remain a word used with children to protect and to guide them. And *no* is one of the words children master saying by the time they are two or three years of age.

Remember the 1980s and 1990s public service announcements that repeated "Just Say No" to prompt us and our children to just say *no* to drugs. The challenge was that being urged to say *no* and actually figuring out how to say *no* in the presence of peer pressure wasn't easy. Nor does it feel easy to us as adults in the workplace or in the relationships that we daily manage. We all struggle with wanting to say *no.* We also struggle to find a safe and appropriate way to say *no* out loud.

The phrase "no more terrorism" has been heard over the airwaves and seen in print repeatedly during the early years of the twenty-first century. So, let's say *no* to all forms of terrorism, violence, and threats of violence. Let's say *no* to drugs. Let's say *no* to drunk driving. Say *no* to domestic violence and to school shootings. Let's also say *no* to frivolous lawsuits and to hostile environments. Say *no* to harassment and to working overtime without pay. Say *no* to the many terror-filled and fear-inspiring situations that we complain about to our family members and friends. And let's even say *no* to children's temper tantrums.

Sometimes you are ready, and *no* is what you actually say out loud.

Sometimes you aren't ready to say *no* and you say nothing. Still other times, you really do want to say *no*, and yet remain silent—in effect giving others the idea that you don't care or that you are actually saying "yes" or "it's okay." The problem is that we now live in a cultural era in which adults are conditioned to say *yes* to maintain an image of being a team player. For more than a decade, time management workshop attendees have spoken variations on this theme: "I can't say *no* at work, I'll lose my job."

One day, I heard a depressed-sounding woman repeat the refrain, "You just don't understand, I can't say *no* at work." My self-protection alarms began to sound. I reasoned, if she can't say *no* at work, can she say *no* at home? And if she can't say *no* at home, what happens when she's taken advantage of during a shopping trip or during a walk in the park? This alarming realization that people are feeling so powerless caused me to spend more time in my time management workshops on the topics of setting priorities and on recognizing when to say *no*. This also caused me to start recording the ways people say *no* in a variety of settings. (You'll find examples throughout the book and in Appendix C.) *No* is not a bad word. In fact, sometimes *no* is the most honest, reasonable and ethical response that a situation calls for. (More on the ethics of *no* in Chapter 4.)

People who fail to say *no* are failing to stand up for their well-being and are really communicating this message: "I'll do whatever you want." Will you really do whatever someone else wants? Consider what your answer or response would be in these situations:

1. Would you give me one of your children just because I asked?

2. Would you let me move into your house just because I asked?

3. Would you happily take on the work of the three people who just quit or were let go?

4. Would you smile as you hand over your car keys because you want to be a team player?

5. Would you quietly go along with a total stranger to a place you've never been?

Not fair questions? These are all fair questions because many of us are being asked questions like these every day. In some of the above situations, did you hesitate for a moment, wanting to utter the words: "It depends"? Did you want more information before making a decision? In the chapters ahead you'll learn how to apply the Power of No Model to collect more information so that you can make clear decisions.

We survived our own terrible twos, threes, and teenage years by saying *no* to everything and everyone, even though *no* was not what children were supposed to say. For many adults, *no* is a word reserved for parents speaking to children.

So as adults, we're conditioned to say *yes*. What a conflict; we want to say *no* and yet find ourselves saying *yes*. Often we say *yes* without getting enough information to make the best possible decision. *Yes* is a powerful word. It has a time, a place, and thousands of appropriate uses. In many places, we've turned into *yes* economies. "Yes, let me buy more. Yes, let me give my kids more than I had. Yes, you can go to the party. Yes, you can do it all. Yes, we'll go on an expensive vacation. Yes, you've just gotten your driver's license and we'll buy you a car. Yes, we should rent a storage space to store some of our belongings that don't fit in the house. Yes, we'll deliver double-digit growth. Yes, we can make more custom products. Yes we can double our workload. Yes, we can improve profit margins for shareholders." And so we go on saying *yes*.

We are conditioned from childhood to say *yes*. When family members want our attention, we want to say *yes*. When employers expect us to say *yes*, we do. And when coworkers ask for help, we want to be nice and help out. The trouble is that when we say *yes* to everyone else, we have little left of our sanity, our personal time, and our energy. When we say *yes* so much that we can't remember saying *no*, the *yes-ism disease* has taken hold in our lives.

The society we live in poses daily "say *yes*" dilemmas. These pretending-to-be-urgent dilemmas—answer the phone, pick up the cell-phone call, return the voicemail message, answer the page, reply to the e-mail, or return the fax with a signature—plague us daily. Yet, how many of these demands on our attention are really worthy of our attention? And how many of these daily demands could we actually say *no* to? Even if you've just replied "not many," that too is okay. Begin to imagine what you could save time for, save energy for, and protect yourself and others from if you'd say *no* even once a day. Imagine the life you might protect by setting a boundary by saying *no*.

## POWER PRACTICE: **ACTIVITIES HARD TO SAY *NO* TO**

Consider where you have the most difficulty saying *no*. Until you recognize the times and places where you are challenged, you can't overcome your waffling and yes-ism behaviors.

1. What activities or projects do you have trouble saying *no* to?

2. What activities or projects do you wish you could say *no* to?

3. To whom is it difficult to say *no*?

4. When are your weakest moments?

5. When is the time you know that you are least likely to say *no* when you need to say *no*?


## Saying No to Friends and Family

Do you find yourself saying *yes* to every request from friends and family in order to keep others happy? And do you end up feeling happy? Many of us have grown accustomed to the idea that saying *yes* to requests does keep others happy. Yet, recall the times *yes* backfired and committed you to doing things you didn't want to do.

At the same time, recall all of the times you've uttered or shouted: "*No*, don't touch. *No*, don't cross the street. *No* throwing the ball in the house. *No* teasing your sister. *No*, you can't play until your room is clean and your homework is done." We say *no* to our children to keep them safe and to set boundaries. Yet as adults, interacting with adults, we fail to set boundaries to keep ourselves safe and sane.

Think about the times you have said *yes* to spending time with family and friends when what you really wanted was to spend a day alone. Your *yes* may have become everyone's pain if your presence was unhappy, agitated, or crabby. Therefore, your *yes* may have left everyone unhappy. Maintaining relationships at home and at work is a challenge if you never say "no."

In the heat of a moment, someone else's excitement, a pleading look, a begging voice, or a combination of these "please say *yes*" tactics can make even a certain *no* melt into a *yes*. What causes you to melt into saying *yes* when you would prefer to say *no*? For some of us, being tired causes us to avoid the word *no*. For others, the eight or more times of hearing someone begging or saying "please!" causes us to melt. And for others, the fear of the consequences of saying *no* drives us to say *yes*. Some people who say *yes* all of the time at work overuse *no* at home. The key is to say *yes* when you mean it, *no* when you mean it, and then to stick to your answers so that others don't second-guess you or renegotiate your every answer.

## Saying No *in the Workplace*

Even at work, a coworker's begging or a boss' demand can cause us to waiver. Over the course of recorded human interactions, each culture reflects expectations for people to say yes more than they say no. And in the last twenty-five years, we've been coached and trained to turn every *no* into a *yes* during business negotiations too. Workplace phrases such as "Don't say *no*, be a team player. How late did you want me to stay? And how many other people's work did you want me to do?" push us toward saying *yes* to everything so that we can keep our jobs, get promised raises, and provide more for ourselves and our families.

Our say-yes behaviors drive the economy, and drive our workplace experiences. Books, videos, and bosses prod us to master saying *yes* and getting others to say *yes*. When what we really need is the healthy balance of saying *yes* and saying *no* appropriately. For instance, contrary to a popular book title, the customer is *not* always right. Saying that the customer is always right means we can't say *no*. If customers are always right, why do companies still have product return policies that require a receipt? Customers, coworkers, and bosses are *not* always right. As a result, recognizing when to say *no* needs to become a part of our daily work life.

Witness the ongoing need in the workplace for whistle-blowers—people who say, "This isn't right." Whistle-blowers bring perceived "wrongs" to the attention of others and even into the court system for correction. If everything happening in the workplace was right and worthy of being said *yes* to, we would not continue to need whistle-blowers. The point is that you need to say *no* in the workplace for the same reasons children need to hear *no*—to ensure safety, to set boundaries, and to help good decision making happen.

## POWER PRACTICE: **SAYING NO**

You've thought about when you've said *yes* and when you have difficulty saying *no*. Now think about the times you wanted to say *no* and actually did say *no*.

1. If you can remember the last time you said *no*, how did it go?

2. What happened? Did a war of words with a child ensue? Did a workplace negotiation take place?

3. How did you feel saying *no*?

4. How did you feel after you said *no*?

5. Did your *no* hold? What happened?

6. Was *no* the right thing to have said? Why?

# THE POWER OF NO SELF-ASSESSMENT

It is time to stop hesitating on decisions, time to stop waffling, and time to be decisive. It is time to claim the power of *no*. When we say *yes* to everything and everyone, we end up loosing ourselves, our time, and in some cases our lives. When we say *yes* to every request and demand, we become our own worst enemies. And we make ourselves victims of our constant decisions to say *yes*. When we fail to say *no* to others, they are in effect invited to turn *on* us. And they can feel invited to do to us, without us, or for us things that we do not want done.

The Power of No Self-Assessment offers you a check-up on your ability to say *no*. The Power of No Self-Assessment tells you whether your reputation and your well-being are at risk. Unmade decisions may cause missed opportunities that do put you or your company, or your family, at risk. Individuals and groups who don't make decisions are called Wafflers.

So, enough on why you need to say *no*. If you've read this far, you are ready to learn how to say *no*. And if you're tired of waffling or *yes*-ism and ready for a change, it's time to master saying *no*. Take the following self-assessment to discover what your typical ability to say *no* really is.

Respond to the Power of No Self-Assessment to discover whether you are a:

- Master of No (you can say *no* effectively now)
- Waffler (you mostly say *maybe*)
- Yes-ism person (you usually say *yes*)

By taking the self-assessment, you'll also discover what messages you tend to rely on: *no-never, mostly maybe,* or *usually yes*. Use this self-assessment to learn about yourself and whether you say *no, maybe,* or *yes* most of the time.

*Table 1-1. The Power of No Self-Assessment*

**Responding Directions**

1. Picture yourself in any of the situations in which you have actually said *no* or have had an opportunity to say *no*.

2. As you read each of the twenty-one statements or questions, consider whether you often say these very words or something similar. If you say it often, put a mark in the Strongly Agree box. If you don't say the words often or at all, put a mark in the Strongly Disagree box. And if you neither strongly agree nor strongly disagree, consider which "Mildly" statement best fits. Be sure you end up with just 21 marks.

| I often find myself saying something similar to: | Strongly Agree | Mildly Agree | Mildly Disagree | Strongly Disagree |
|---|---|---|---|---|
| 1. No. | | | | |
| 2. Couldn't you find someone else? | | | | |
| 3. My schedule is full right now, try me in a few months. | | | | |
| 4. I could do that if you can't find anyone else. | | | | |
| 5. My schedule doesn't allow me to take that on right now. | | | | |
| 6. No way. | | | | |
| 7. No thank you. | | | | |
| 8. I'm sorry I can't help out. | | | | |
| 9. I'm willing to serve. | | | | |
| 10. What part of *no* don't you understand? | | | | |
| 11. I don't think I'm the best person for this. | | | | |
| 12. I could probably help out. | | | | |
| 13. My schedule doesn't allow me to take that on at all. | | | | |
| 14. Maybe later. | | | | |
| 15. I'd be happy to. | | | | |
| 16. I won't do that at all. | | | | |
| 17. Maybe. | | | | |
| 18. How can I help? | | | | |
| 19. Stop. Don't do that. | | | | |
| 20. I think I've already taken on too much. | | | | |
| 21. Yes. | | | | |

## *Table 1-2. Scoring the Power-of-No Self-Assessment*

**Scoring Directions**

1.  For each of the twenty-one items, transfer your responses by circling the number in the corresponding level of agreement column on the scoring grid that follows.

2.  After you have circled 21 numbers (one for each item), add the numbers together for a grand total.

3.  Locate your grand total in the Results Grid below and learn how well you really say *no*.

4.  Then read the section titled "What the Self-Assessment Tells Us" to learn more about yourself and others.

## *Results Grid*

| *If your point total is:* | *When it comes to saying no, you are a:* |
|---|---|
| 63–77 | **Master of No:** You can say *no* graciously and effectively whenever you choose. |
| 42–62 | **Waffler:** You can't say *no* and can't say *yes* clearly, so mostly you say *maybe*. |
| 23–41 | **Yes-ism Person**—You usually say *yes*. |

| I often find myself saying something similar to: | Strongly Agree | Mildly Agree | Mildly Disagree | Strongly Disagree |
|---|---|---|---|---|
| **Sample** | | | | |
| 1. No. | 4 | 3 | 2 | 1 |
| 1. No. | 4 | 3 | 2 | 1 |
| 2. Couldn't you find someone else? | 1 | 2 | 3 | 3 |
| 3. My schedule is full right now, try me in a few months. | 1 | 2 | 3 | 3 |
| 4. I could do that if you can't find anyone else. | 1 | 2 | 3 | 3 |
| 5. My schedule doesn't allow me to take that on right now. | 2 | 2 | 1 | 1 |
| 6. No way. | 4 | 3 | 2 | 1 |
| 7. No thank you. | 4 | 3 | 2 | 1 |
| 8. I'm sorry I can't help out. | 2 | 2 | 3 | 3 |
| 9. I'm willing to serve. | 1 | 2 | 3 | 3 |
| 10. What part of *no* don't you understand? | 3 | 3 | 2 | 1 |
| 11. I don't think I'm the best person for this. | 3 | 2 | 2 | 2 |
| 12. I could probably help out. | 1 | 2 | 3 | 4 |
| 13. My schedule doesn't allow me to take that on at all. | 4 | 3 | 2 | 1 |
| 14. Maybe later. | 1 | 2 | 3 | 3 |
| 15. I'd be happy to. | 1 | 2 | 3 | 4 |
| 16. I won't do that at all. | 4 | 3 | 2 | 1 |
| 17. Maybe. | 1 | 1 | 3 | 3 |
| 18. How can I help? | 1 | 2 | 3 | 4 |
| 19. Stop. Don't do that. | 4 | 3 | 2 | 1 |
| 20. I think I've already taken on too much. | 1 | 1 | 3 | 3 |
| 21. Yes. | 1 | 2 | 3 | 4 |

Power-of-No Grand Total _____

## WHAT THE POWER OF NO SELF-ASSESSMENT TELLS US

The qualities demonstrated by people at each of these levels of ability to say *no* are distinct. As you took the self-assessment, you likely recognized phrases and statements that you use and that people you know well use on a regular basis. Identifying what you typically say allows you to recognize how others perceive your ability to say *no*.

Again, the twenty-one questions help you identify whether your say-no-approach is a:

> Master of No (you can say *no* effectively now)
> Waffler (you mostly say *maybe*)
> Yes-ism person (you usually say *yes*)

The Power of No Self-Assessment sheds light on the three ability-to-say-no levels or say-no approaches that you use with varying degrees of success and varying degrees of consistency. We all say *yes* and we all say *no*. The key is to maximize your ability to say *no* appropriately and to recognize when others are trying to tell you *no* and don't know how.

Each of the twenty-one phrases also relates to the three primary messages: *no—never*, mostly *maybe*, or usually *yes*. Here's how the numbered self-assessment statements match up to these three styles of saying *no*.

- *No, Never.* The Masters of No often say no in these ways:

  1. No.
  6. No way.
  7. No thank you.
  10. What part of no don't you understand?
  13. My schedule doesn't allow me to take that on at all.
  16. I won't do that at all.
  19. Stop. Don't do that.

- *No, Maybe Later.* The Wafflers live here, mostly saying *maybe* in these or similar ways:

  2. Couldn't you find someone else?
  5. My schedule doesn't allow me to take that on right now.
  8. I'm sorry I can't help out.
  11. I don't think I'm the best person for this.

14. Maybe later.
17. Maybe.
20. I think I've already taken on too much.

- *No, Not Now. I'll Say Yes Later.* Yes-ism people live here, usually saying *yes* in these or similar ways:

    3. My schedule is full right now, try me in a few months.
    4. I could do that if you can't find anyone else.
    9. I'm willing to serve.
    12. I could probably help out.
    15. I'd be happy to.
    18. How can I help?

## WHAT ALL THIS MEANS

To better understand each of the three skill levels and approaches for saying *no*, keep reading. In the descriptions for each of the three skill levels that follow, you'll see six paragraphs. Each paragraph describes a different aspect for understanding yourself and others. Whether you are a Master of No, a Waffler, or a Yes-ism person, you have an opportunity to improve your skills and to better understand what others are telling you, and what others need from you to help them make a more effective decision. You'll see the following six descriptive paragraphs for each of the three say-no approaches.

- *Qualities*: This paragraph describes how you might recognize yourself or someone else with this approach to saying *no*.

- *Upsides*: This paragraph outlines the strengths of the listed approach to saying *no*.

- *Downsides*: This paragraph outlines the weaknesses or potential limitations of the say-no approach you're reading about.

- *To Be More Effective, Consider*: When this is your primary say-no approach to saying *no*, this paragraph suggests how you might interact more effectively with others.

- *When You Have a Different Say-No Approach*: To interact more effectively with someone who relies on this approach to saying *no*, use the tips in this paragraph.

• *Some Cautions*: This paragraph shares some things to be aware of in yourself.

## THE SAY-NO APPROACHES DEFINED

### 1. As a Master of No (you can say no *effectively now*)

• *Qualities*: We recognize the Masters of No by their directness and their comfort with saying *no*. There's *no* hesitation, *no* waffling, and *no* apology. A Master of No takes ownership for her choice and response. A Master of No is gracious in his word choice and message delivery. A Master of No has an often unrealistic expectation that others can be equally clear about when to say *no*. A Master of No knows how and when to say *no* and to say *yes*.

• *Upsides*: Masters of No are clear, direct, and decisive. There is never a question about whether the speaker really meant *no*.

• *Downsides*: Because of their directness, Masters of No can be perceived as cold, uncaring, not helpful, and as not willing to be part of a team. Some Masters of No have also been described as aloof, too good for everyone else, and hard to get to know.

• *To Be More Effective, Consider*: When you are a Master of No, consider carefully the speed of your delivery, the tone of your voice, and words you use to say *no*. Everyone hears your *no* differently. The key is to say *no* in such a way that you are clear and concise without sounding critical of others or sounding mean and rude.

• *When You Have a Different Say-No Approach*: When you are dealing with others who are Masters of No, be more direct when you ask questions and when you respond to questions. No waffling. When you waffle, a Master of No sees you as indecisive and sometimes as weak.

• *Some Cautions*: As a Master of No, be patient with yourself and others. Most people can't yet say *no* as effectively as you do. Your ability to say *no* may endear you to some, or it may alienate you from others. Saying *no* with tact, grace, and elegance is an art to continually improve and master. When you see others struggling in their ability to say *no*, offer to help them clarify their position by applying The Power of No Model described in Chapter 2.

### 2. As a Waffler (you mostly say maybe)

• *Qualities*: Wafflers want to give the best possible answer, yet feel that they don't have enough information to make a decision. Wafflers can also want to avoid making a decision because they believe that avoiding a decision keeps them safe or liked.

- *Upsides*: Wafflers are rarely considered rude.

- *Downsides*: Wafflers are often considered weak, incompetent, or slow.

- *To Be More Effective, Consider*: Learning as quickly as possible all the models approaches, questions, tips, and strategies in this book.

- *When You Have a Different Say-No Approach*: Help the Wafflers get the information they need to make a decision, prompt them with Power of No questions. Be patient while they improve their skills.

- *Some Cautions*: As a Waffler, you'll want to find a skilled Master of No to learn from. To Masters of No, Wafflers can appear weak, indecisive, and worthy of being left behind. When you want to say *no*, need to say *no*, or feel that *no* is the best response, then remember to say *no*.

## 3. As a Yes-ism Person (you usually say yes)

- *Qualities*: We recognize Yes-ism people because they say *yes* to everything. Some are loved for this. However, because they say *yes* to everything, many of the things they say *yes* to don't happen. So, some people are also very unhappy.

- *Upsides*: Yes-ism people are seen as a people who want to be helpful. Others rely on Yes-ism people for a lot of things.

- *Downsides*: Yes-ism people don't have much time for themselves. All the things committed to don't get done. Yes-ism people often beat themselves up for not getting everything done.

- *To Be More Effective, Consider*: Learning, as quickly as possible, all the models, approaches, questions, tips, and strategies in this book.

- *When You Have a Different Say-No Approach*: Clarify whether the person saying *yes* will actually follow through on the commitment being made. Help the Yes-ism person pause and ask questions to determine whether *yes* or *no* is the best response. Be patient while they move improve their skills.

- *Some Cautions*: As a Yes-ism person, stop feeling obligated to say *yes*. Find a Master of No to learn from. If you keep saying *yes* and getting things done, you'll continually be asked to do more. Find a balance of personal, professional, and community involvement that inspires you, and allows you to complete your commitments without wearing yourself out or short-changing the people important to you.

Can we rely on one say-no approach at work and another at home? Yes, we can and do because different environments and people in those environments expect different behaviors and approaches from us. At work you may be expected to say *yes* and be a team player, while at home you may be a disciplinarian and find yourself having to say *no*. Or, at home you may be the go-to-person-because-I-know-I-always-get-a-*yes*-from-you, while at work you are the-buck-stops-here-person who says *no* to projects and people.

## POWER PRACTICE: RECOGNIZE THE SAY-NO APPROACHES

For each of the following twenty items, identify the say-no approach represented. Circle your answer for each item. (Answers are upside down following the exercise.)

| | |
|---|---|
| 1. No. | *Master of No, Waffler, or Yes-ism person* |
| 2. Maybe. | *Master of No, Waffler, or Yes-ism person* |
| 3. Yes. | *Master of No, Waffler, or Yes-ism person* |
| 4. No, I'm not going to be able to join you. I'm sorry, I wish I could. | *Master of No, Waffler, or Yes-ism person* |
| 5. I don't think we can come to the party. | *Master of No, Waffler, or Yes-ism person* |
| 6. I'd like to come to the show. Thank you for inviting me. (And you really do want to go.) | *Master of No, Waffler, or Yes-ism person* |
| 7. Stop doing that to your sister. Your behavior is unacceptable. | *Master of No, Waffler, or Yes-ism person* |
| 8. Would you please stop doing that. I'm sure your sister doesn't like it when you do that. | *Master of No, Waffler, or Yes-ism person* |
| 9. No. My project schedule is full and I won't add a new project. | *Master of No, Waffler, or Yes-ism person* |

| | |
|---|---|
| 10. Sure, I can help you on that project. | *Master of No, Waffler, or Yes-ism person* |
| 11. I don't know if I can fit that in. | *Master of No, Waffler, or Yes-ism person* |
| 12. No, I'd rather not. | *Master of No, Waffler, or Yes-ism person* |
| 13. I'm ready. Let's go. | *Master of No, Waffler, or Yes-ism person* |
| 14. Can you wait for me? | *Master of No, Waffler, or Yes-ism person* |
| 15. No, I'm not leaving now. | *Master of No, Waffler, or Yes-ism person* |
| 16. I'm not quite ready to go. Can you give me two minutes? | *Master of No, Waffler, or Yes-ism person* |
| 17. I guess this will be all right. | *Master of No, Waffler, or Yes-ism person* |
| 18. Stop. Let me out. | *Master of No, Waffler, or Yes-ism person* |
| 19. Let me out. I want to get home with someone else. | *Master of No, Waffler, or Yes-ism person* |
| 20. Sounds good. Let's move ahead. | *Master of No, Waffler, or Yes-ism person* |

*Answers:*
1. Master of No  2. Waffler  3. Master of No  4. Master of No
5. Waffler  6. Master of No  7. Master of No  8. Waffler
9. Master of No  10. Yes-ism person  11. Waffler  12. Waffler
13. Master of No  14. Yes-ism person  15. Master of No  16. Waffler
17. Waffler  18. Master of No  19. Waffler  20. Master of No

## SAY-NO APPROACHES USE SAY-NO MESSAGES

We've defined three say-no approaches and related behaviors for saying *no*. Again, the three messages that each of the three say-no approaches rely on are:

1. *No—Never.* The Masters can say *no*. We'll explore these messages more in Chapter 5.

2. *No—Maybe later.* The Wafflers live here, mostly saying *maybe*. We'll explore these messages more in Chapter 6.

3. *No—Not now, I'll say yes later* (which may be in just a minute). The Yes-ism people live here. We'll explore these messages more in Chapter 7.

## THE BOTTOM LINE

We've conditioned and backed ourselves, our children, coworkers, bosses, and friends into saying *yes* more than *no*. We can rephrase the last two decades of "Just say *no* to drugs" into the phrase for this millennium "Stop waffling and claim the power to say no." Yet, telling ourselves to say *no* is not enough. Finding the words we'll use to say *no* and following through on our resolve is sometimes just as difficult as making the decision to say *no* is in the first place.

You can overcome Yes-ism and give-up being a Waffler to become a Master of No. You can refine your decision-making skills to become a Master of No. As a Master of No, you can improve your skills in coaching individuals and groups through improved decision-making.:

## POWER SUMMARY

1. You know what your say-no approach skill level is: Master of No, Waffler, or Yes-ism person.

2. You know what your preferred say-no messages are: "No, never," "No, *maybe*," or "No, not now. *Yes* later."

3. *No* is an important, legitimate, and needed word.

4. Be decisive. Stop waffling.

## CHAPTER 2

# The Power of No

*No* Is Just as Important as *Yes*

**POWER PREVIEW POINTS**

1. Understand the Power of No Model for decision making.
2. Learn to ask questions that help you make a *yes* or *no* decision.

In this chapter you will learn about the Power of No Model, which will help you make clear yes or no decisions. The word "power" in this book means "having an ability to act or to cause an effect." The Power of No Model will help you control your own choices and life. With the power you gain from the model, you will be able to carefully and positively to set boundaries that protect yourself and others. The model is a tool for learning to say *no* more easily and quickly. *No* is just as important as *yes*. This is proven by the number of people who are desperate to learn to say *no*. So, how can you learn to say *no* when you really want to, need to, or feel compelled to? How can you say *no* without alienating yourself from others, losing your job, or breaking apart your relationships? *The answer is* the Power of No Model™. Practice with the model so that you can say *no* every time you want to.

## THE POWER OF NO MODEL

Use the Power of No Model to turn your internal *no* into a spoken out loud *no*. The key to success when saying *no* is to say the word *no* firmly and in a manner that others will hear and take seriously.

The Power of No Model is made up of five decision points that are easily remembered by the acronym POWER:

**P**urpose
**O**ptions/Resources
**W**hen
**E**motional Ties
**R**ights and Responsibilities.

These five decision-points include subsets of questions, conversations, and agreements that will lead you to say *yes* and to say *no* when it is most fitting. These subsets of discussion will also help you to protect yourself and others as you determine whether you'll say *yes* or *no* to a request, an invitation, or a demand. Once you've learned to apply the Power of No Model, it takes just a few minutes to apply and to use in a conversation.

## Purpose

The purpose of a request is the statement of what is wanted or needed, why it is wanted, and how it relates to the goals to be accomplished. Understanding the purpose of a request is always the place to start. Consider whether the purpose is safe or dangerous. In other words, is the purpose related to the organization's goals, to your goals, or to your family's goals, and does it promote or hurt your well-being? A safe purpose helps you to achieve goals and to protect your well-being and the well-being of your family.

Is the request dangerous? In other words, does the request conflict with the goals or demands of your business, with your personal goals, values, and priorities, or with your important relationships? A dangerous request may actually put you at risk. A dangerous or threatening purpose is *no*t in your best interest and may be something as simple as a request that is not a good use of your time.

Early in the development of my company, I found myself asking people who called to invite me to lunch why they wanted to meet with me. I wanted to protect my time and my physical well-being. And I wanted to avoid meetings that would require more time than I could spend if the meeting's purpose had to do with them selling me something or with only getting someone else's needs met. So, I was direct and always asked what the purpose of the meeting would be. When sharing this story during time management workshops, participants have said that this sounds rather cold (which is how Masters of No sometimes do sound) and that they couldn't imagine being so reasoned and logical as to require a clear purpose for a lunch meeting.

Yet, don't we all do that? When someone calls, don't you wonder "what does this person want?" and sometimes ask out loud, "how may I help you?" Asking how you can help someone is all about defining a purpose. So, when you answer the phone, make a lunch appointment, schedule a meeting, or agree to see a family member, it is all about knowing the purpose of the planned interaction. Purpose can range from making a sale, spending quality social time, supporting a family member, completing a project, or exploring a new opportunity, to ending an exploration or a relationship. Unless you know the purpose of a request, how can you prepare a response? Until you know the purpose of a project, how can you begin to identify whether it is a project that fits the business' goals?

Until you know the purpose of an interaction, how can you assess whether it is safe or dangerous to keep going? Once you recognize a dangerous purpose, you can immediately say *no*, stand your ground, and move on. Being clear about requests for your time can help keep you safe and productive.

When you recognize a safe purpose, you can explore further whether you want to, or should, pursue the invitation or request. Sometimes you can recognize a safe purpose and yet still wonder what exactly the request involves. When safety is established, you can invest more time to help the requester to clearly define what is needed. Ask questions such as, "What needs to be done? What does the finished product need to look like? And what goal does it help us to accomplish?"

When you recognize the purpose and the scope of a request that sounds like you could say *yes*, the next step in the Power of No Model is to discover what options and resources are available to help accomplish the request.

## POWER PRACTICE: DEFINE THE PURPOSE OF A REQUEST

1. Next time someone asks you for help, how will you uncover the purpose of the request? For example, you could ask: "What would you like help with? What will doing this help us accomplish?"

What will you ask?

2. What will you do? What questions will you ask? For example, you could politely and calmly ask: "What do you want me to do?"

What will you ask?

3. How will you behave? For example, will you be angry, calm, loud, soft-spoken, direct or indirect?

4. What will you ask to determine the size and scope of the request or to determine what the expected result of the project is? For example, you could ask: "What do you want the finished project to look like?"

What will you ask?


Purpose also has to do with your personal priorities. What are your core values? What goals are you focused on achieving? What are your highest priorities—family time, career advancement, vacation, health, wealth, peace of mind, or what? Be very clear about what is important to you so that you can weigh each request, invitation, and question with your personal purpose in mind. Filter everything through the purpose-defining step, getting clear on what is being asked of you, and then holding the request up in the light of what your personal purpose is. If there is a match, you can move on to the second decision-point of the Power of No Model. If there isn't a match, you know right now that you need to say *no* to the opportunity being presented.

## Options and Resources

Now that you understand the purpose of the request, it is time to find out what options and resources are available to you.

*Options* are what you choose from to get things done. Options are about how you get things done. Options are the choices available to you to accomplish the purpose of a request and to make decisions about how the request will be accomplished. For example, will you hire someone or do the project yourself?

*Resources* are about what and who is available to help get things done. Resources are the tools, people, equipment, finances, and authority-levels available to help complete the request. You might be the only resource or you might have volunteers, family members, or team members who can help.

Ask questions such as these to explore what options and resources really are available to you:

- Can someone else take on the assignment?
- How many ways can the task be completed?
- What tools, equipment and money will be available to help complete the request?

- Who is available to help? How many volunteers or workers can help? Have they done this kind of work before or will they need training?

A project, invitation, or proposal may sound good. However, until you discover what options and resources are available for the completion of the request, how can you know how realistic the request is? The reality is, you can't. So spend as much time as possible learning what options and resources will be committed and delivered to help you achieve the request.

If the options and resources available to you don't allow for a successful result, now is the time to say *no*. If options and resources are available to help get things done, it's time to move on to the next decision-point and discover when the project or action is due.

## POWER PRACTICE: DISCOVER YOUR OPTIONS AND RESOURCES

1. Once you know what the purpose of the request is, how will you learn what options and resources are available to you?

2. How do you envision completing the project? What methods and processes will you use?

3. Do you already know what you'll need to complete the project? If not, start a list of what you'll need.

4. Who will you need to help you complete the project? Are they available?

### When

A statement of when a request needs to be completed tells you the timing of the project, or the time frame of the request for help. A "when" statement establishes a clear deadline for the request. To determine when the request needs to be done, ask for a specific date and time when the project, task, committee assignment, or honey-please-do-this list-item is to be completed. Ask whether it is a fixed and non-negotiable deadline or a negotiable or floating deadline. Discover whether the timing of the request fits in with what you have already prioritized to do. Will the timing of this request allow for the needed resources to be available as planned? Can you negotiate the deadline?

If someone says "as soon as possible" in response to your question of when the request needs to be done, consider the response as a non-response. Why? Because, to the person asking the question, "as soon as possible" may mean in the next ten minutes, in the next two days, or in the next two months. How do you know what the requester is asking? Be persistent and ask again, "when does this really need to be done?" You are looking for a deadline that includes a date, a time, and in some cases, a time zone.

For instance, an effective statement of a deadline, when you are working across time zones, would be "I'd like the project to be completed by noon, Pacific Time, on February 17, 2005." This clear deadline statement includes a time, a time-zone, a month, date, and a year. "Please get this back to me by 2 P.M. today" is also clear. These deadlines leave no doubt as to when the requester expects to see the finished project.

Identifying the clear deadline is in everyone's best interest. Having a deadline protects your time, your team's time, your work time, and your personal time. A noble or well-defined purpose, supported by options and resources, and yet requested without a deadline or with an unrealistic time frame is a request worthy of a *no*. In other words, the question of when something needs to be done is another potential stop-or-go decision-point. The question of "When?" is answered with a fixed, floating, or negotiable date and time. Discover which deadline you've been given before going on.

A well-defined purpose, supported by options, resources, and a clear and realistic deadline is potentially a request to which you'll say *yes*. However, the fourth decision-point, emotional ties, may change your response to a *no*.

## POWER PRACTICE: DEFINE WHEN THE REQUEST IS DUE

1. The next time someone says "as soon as possible," what will you say?

2. The next time someone says the deadline is "whenever you can get to it," what will you say?

3. The next time someone says, "Honey, will you please clean the garage this weekend," what will you say?

4. The next time someone promises to "have this done for you on Monday," what will you say?

5. What questions will you ask to clarify when the requester wants things done?

Even when the definitions for the Purpose, Options, and When of the project are clear, you're not really safe yet in making a *yes* or a *no* commitment. There are two more decision-points to visit and discuss. Consider how you feel about making a commitment and agree on what your rights and responsibilities are.

## Emotional Ties

Saying *no* is both a logical and an emotional process. Emotions can grow from your past experiences, from your intuitive sense of how the project or request will work out, or from an unexplained sense of not wanting to do something. Emotions converge on you without your asking them to. Emotions may prompt excitement, commitment, and energy for saying *yes* to a request. On the other hand, emotions may prompt resentment, distrust, and energy for saying *no* to a request. Emotions can prompt you to say "no," or leave me alone," or "get out of here" so quickly that you don't realize what has happened. When this rapid, almost instinctive response to say *no* takes over, trust it.

An immediate and seemingly-without-reason urge to say *no* comes from your emotional ties to a situation, a person, a group, or environment. The strong urge to say *no* is a form of protection. A "bad feeling" or a "gut feeling" may prompt you to say *no*. Emotions can be good ("I feel good about this"), bad ("I feel something bad will happen"), neutral ("I don't care"), or mixed ("I'm not sure").

The first three decision-points—Purpose, Options, and When—are logical. You reason through each of them, negotiating where needed. Yet, even with all that logical discussion, emotions can affect whether you'll actually commit to saying yes or no.

After you look at each request clearly and thoroughly, consider how you feel. What is it that you really want to do, to accomplish, or want to be involved with? Beware of letting others force you into doing things you don't feel like doing. Protect yourself, your well-being, and your time by listening to your emotional responses to questions and invitations.

Ask yourself how you will feel if you say *no*. And consider how you will feel if you say *yes*? Then determine what your best response to a request really is.

## POWER PRACTICE: RECOGNIZE YOUR EMOTIONS

1. When was the last time you said *no* so quickly that you didn't realize that you'd said *no*?

2.  What emotions or past experience prompted your reaction?

3.  What emotions will guide you to say *no* to a request?

4.  What emotions will lead you to say *yes* to a request?

5.  Who can you turn to for insight when your emotions and your logic are in conflict?

## Rights and Responsibilities

With every *yes* or *no* decision you make, consider what your rights and responsibilities are.

**Rights.** Rights are the things that can be claimed as true about a situation and the things that will continue to be true whether you say *yes* or *no* to a request. During a rights decision-point discussion, you can confirm whether the request is reasonable and legal.

You can ask what rights you will have if you say *yes*. For instance, at work you can ask, "What resources have been committed and will not be taken away? Who is available that won't be reassigned in such a way that I'll lose their help? What authority will I have that won't be taken away during the project?"

At home, you'll ask what commitments will be kept without fail. Ask what you can expect to have protected, whether it is time together, time alone, and or time watching the kids. When the answers about rights and expectations at home are not clear, ask kindly for more information.

Also, ask what rights you will have if you say *no*. For instance, what will happen to your current and future project opportunities if you say *no*, how will you be treated if you say *no*, or what consequences will you face if you say *no*? When the answers are not clear, ask the people you work with, the people you volunteer with, and the people you live with for clarification of what you can expect.

**Responsibilities.** Along with your rights, learn what responsibilities you will be accountable for. Responsibilities are the legal, moral, or mental accountabilities or duties that you will be expected to live up to, deliver on, and perform to. For example, your responsibility when you say *yes* to a project is to stay within or under the budget for project expenses, or to find a baby-sitter to watch the children for five hours so that you and your spouse can spend an evening together. Clarifying the responsibilities that go with saying *yes* to a request protects you because it prevents confusion and frustration.

When you say *no*, you are not necessarily relieved of responsibility.

Saying *no* may mean that you need to tell other people what has changed, or where help can be found so that the project or activity can still be completed without you.

## POWER PRACTICE: DEFINE YOUR RIGHTS AND RESPONSIBILITIES

1. What words will you use to ask your boss about your rights on a project? For example, "What can I realistically expect when I'm looking for help on this project?"

2. What words will you use to ask your team leader about your responsibilities on a project? For example, "What are your expectations of me as I work on this project?"

3. What words will you use to confirm your responsibilities to your family? For example, "What are your expectations of me when I'm at home?"

4. What questions will you ask to decide whether you'll serve on a committee? For example, "What does the committee chair expect the time commitment to be?"

The five decision-points for reaching a clear *yes* or *no* answer end with the clarification of your rights and responsibilities. You might have thought you'd say *yes* up until this point, when you learn that you are expected to chair the committee you have been asked to serve on. According to Vickie Holbrook, managing editor of the *Idaho Press-Tribune*:

> Often, it's a form of compromise. Instead of serving on a committee, I offer to brainstorm or meet once or twice with a group or a couple of people from the committee. I ask several questions. "What kind of commitment are you asking for? Are you expecting me to be a leader or a participant?" I tell people what I can do or what I'm willing to do. I try to set the parameters and define very clearly what I can and can't do.

Vickie's question-asking and boundary-setting on a request are all about defining the rights and responsibilities attached to the request.

# ANOTHER WAY TO LOOK AT THE POWER OF NO MODEL

View the five decision-points for saying *no* in terms of whether they are logical or emotional. The logical elements are Purpose, Options, and When. These items can be discussed, reasoned through, negotiated, and renegotiated. They provide the foundation and base agreements of a request.

Then there are the emotional elements considered in decision-point 4, Emotional Ties. Emotions can run above, around, and through the other four decision-points. They can help or hinder the progress and accomplishment of a request at any time. They demand awareness, attention, and respect because when a lack of care or respect is perceived, emotions can take over and undermine the success of a project or a request.

Rights and Responsibilities are both logical and emotional. Rights come from what you expect and believe, and as such they are both logical and emotional. Responsibilities that are offered to you may inspire you or may depress you; either way you are feeling something about what you have to work with. The rights and responsibilities that you know you need to complete a project may not be agreed to by the requester, in which case it then causes emotional stress and strain. So the logical and the emotional elements weave together to influence decisions, responses, and results.

- *Purpose* tells what needs to be done.
- *Options* and *Resources* tell how you might get it done.
- *When* tells the time-frame for getting things done.
- The *Emotional Ties* tell you how you feel about a request or question.
- *Rights and Responsibilities* have to do with both us and other people, with the what, how, and when logical elements and the feel emotional elements.

So what does all of this mean? The Power of No Model means that you can apply both logic and emotion to every question and invitation that comes your way. The model offers decision-points that can slow down your decision-making processes and provide time and the tools for discussing what makes the most sense to say *yes* to and what to say *no* to. At the same time, the Model prompts you to ask questions that can speed up a decision process when it is stalled or stuck, and a decision is needed.

Think about how you can apply the Power of No Model in team, project, or even family meetings. Begin looking at the kinds of questions you'll use to get information and insight to make your *yes* or *no* decision. The Power Practices throughout the book help you pause, reflect, and record your questions and approaches for improving your decision-making discussions and conclusions.

## POWER PRACTICE: USING THE POWER OF NO MODEL

It's your turn to begin crafting the questions you'll use to get buy-in, recognize when to say *no*, and recognize where negotiations can occur. In order to define each of the five POWER considerations, write down the questions you can use the next time someone asks you to do something. Sample questions follow this opportunity for you to draft your own questions.

**P**urpose

**O**ptions and Resources

**W**hen

**E**motional Ties

**R**ights and Responsibilities

## POTENTIAL POWER QUESTIONS

The list that follows provides examples of questions you could have written for the above Power Practice. These questions can help you, your family, or help your team to define the Purpose, Options and Resources, When, Emotional Ties, and Rights and Responsibilities of any given request so that you can make the best possible decisions together.

**P**urpose
- What is it that needs to be accomplished?
- Whose goals will be served by this project?
- What needs to be done?
- What does the finished product need to look like?

- What goal will we accomplish by doing this?
- What's the budget for this?
- What results are you looking for?
- What has already been done?
- What are the performance criteria?
- What are the specifications?
- What regulations govern this?
- What organizational policies apply to this?
- What's the purpose or goal here?
- How many sales do we have to make to hit this goal?
- Do we need to modify our product offering? How?
- Do we need to create a new product? What?
- How does the direction of our product offerings need to change?
- What does the business need to do next?
- We have no profit, how can we cut expenses?
- What size building can we afford?
- How much can we spend?
- How much will it cost?
- What are we going after here?
- What do we want this to include when it's finished?
- What certifications do we need to have to do this?
- What regulatory agencies will be involved?
- What does our strategic plan say?
- What does our implementation plan say?
- What does the manual say?
- What are the house rules?
- What company policies with respect to customer service, on time delivery, product performance, pricing, environment, natural resources management, and others will affect our decision?
- What part of our planning cycle will affect us?
- How is our decision in line with company strategy?
- What technologies are you familiar with that may emerge as competition?

And the list could go on and on. The same is true for the number of potential questions that could be asked for Options and Resources, When, Emotional Ties, and Rights and Responsibilities. The lists that follow are shorter—for two reasons. One, they are meant as idea-starters, not as the be-all-to-end-all lists. Two, the defining of a Purpose really is the largest task, and therefore more questions should be asked at that decision-point.

Options and Resources
- What options are available to us?

- What resources will be available to do this?
- How should this be done?
- What equipment can be used?
- What tools are available?
- Who's available to help?
- Where can we get the budget to do this?
- Who can we tap as an internal and/or external think tank?
- Who else can do this?
- What is there already in development that can help get this done?
- What technologies are currently available to help?
- Do I have to be included on this?
- How many ways can we approach this?
- How many ways could we get this done?
- Which volunteers can help out?
- What training will the available people need?
- What do you think is the best option?
- What are we overlooking?
- What is missing from our view and consideration?
- What other perspectives can we approach this from?
- Who would see this in a different way?
- How do our customers view this?
- How do our family members want to see this happen?

**W**hen

- What's the deadline?
- Is the deadline fixed or negotiable?
- Can we negotiate when it has to be done?
- What's the penalty if this doesn't get done on time?
- What are the consequences of missing the deadline?
- Will the timing of this allow us to access the needed resources?
- What day is this needed?
- What time is this needed?
- Before the deadline, when can we meet to confirm progress on the project?
- When will the needed resources be available?
- When will staff be available?
- When will you be available?
- When will funds be available?
- When is the drop-dead date?
- When do I have to make a decision?
- When do I have to place the order or make the purchase?
- When do I have to make a deposit?

- How long can we delay?
- What are the consequences of a delay?
- Where can we make up for lost time?
- Where can we save time as we move ahead?
- What can we do to streamline the process so that it moves faster?
- What process improvements will let things run more quickly?

Emotional Ties

These questions you can ask yourself internally. When it is helpful, some of the questions can be asked of others to determine their feelings about moving forward on a request.

- How do you feel about saying *yes*?
- How do you feel about saying *no*?
- How will you feel if the team goes on without you?
- How do other team members feel about this project?
- How will a team member feel about being left out?
- What experience is making you feel this way about this project?
- What emotions are causing this reaction?
- What past experience is prompting this reaction?
- Where will resistance be encountered?
- Who will fight this project?
- Who will stand in the way of this approach?
- What is the cause of the concern?
- How can we overcome the resistance to this?
- How can you cheer the team on?
- How much energy do you feel like investing in this?
- What fears are making you feel uncomfortable about this project?
- What's happening in the environment around you that makes you feel concerned?
- What's happening in the environment around you that makes you feel excited?
- What's happening in the environment around you that makes you feel angry?
- What's happening in the environment around you that makes you feel anxious?
- What's happening in the environment around you that makes you feel comfortable?
- What consequences make you feel _____ (whatever emotion)?
- How will the consequences make you feel?
- Do you really want to be involved in this? Why?
- Do you feel like someone is forcing you to do this?

- What do you feel is the best approach or answer?
- What emotions will guide you to say yes?
- What emotions will guide you to say *no*?
- Who can you turn to for insight?
- Who can you turn to when your emotions and your logic are in conflict?
- Is saying *yes* or *no* the most kind thing to say?

**R**ights and Responsibilities
- What authority will you have to get this done?
- What resources have been committed and will not be taken away?
- Who is available who won't be reassigned and unable to help?
- What authority will you be given that won't be taken away during the project?
- What commitments will be kept without fail?
- What will protect you while you work on this?
- How will you protect your time while you work on this?
- What rights will you have if you say *no*?
- What rights will you have if you say *yes*?
- How will you be treated if you say *no*?
- How will you be treated if you say yes?
- What consequences will you face if you say *no*?
- What consequences will you face if you say *yes*?
- What will you be responsible for if you say yes?
- What will you be responsible for if you say *no*?
- What needs to be clarified that might cause confusion once the project gets started?
- What needs to be protected as you move forward?
- Who needs to be protected as you move forward?
- What kind of commitment are you asking for?
- Are you expecting to be a leader or a participant?
- Is saying *yes* or *no* the most fair thing to say?
- Is saying *yes* or *no* the most honest thing to say?
- Does your response maintain your integrity?
- Does your response reflect the highest good for the situation?

## MAKE A DECISION

The word "decision" comes from the Latin word *decidere,* which means to cut off. The Power of No Model could be described in terms of cutting things off in the following ways:

- **P**urpose. If the purpose is too large, you can narrow its scope or cut out some of the details and the nice-to-have items to make the project more manageable.

- **O**ptions and Resources. When options and resources aren't available, you sometimes hear "we've been cut off" or "I've been cut out of the loop."

- **W**hen. The timing of a request may prevent you from doing other things. So, you are in effect pulled off or cut off from doing other things during the time of the requested project.

- **E**motional Ties. You may honestly listen and respond to how you feel or you may cut yourself off and not listen to your emotions at all.

- **R**ights and Responsibilities. When you feel your rights and responsibilities are being stepped on, limited, abused, or cut off, you tend to walk away from the activity or even quit altogether.

## POWER PRACTICE: MAKING A DECISION

1. When was the last time you made a decision where you felt cut off?

2. Where did the cut-off occur?

> **P**urpose—What happened?
> **O**ptions and Resources—What happened?
> **W**hen—What happened?
> **E**motional Ties—What happened?
> **R**ights and Responsibilities—What happened?

From years of observing who can say *no* most easily and keep smiling, feeling good, and moving on, here's in general what I think tends to happen. More men appear to feel comfortable saying *no* than do women. More women feel comfortable saying *yes* than do men. And the comfort level with saying *maybe*, and therefore behaving like a Waffler, appears to split fairly evenly between men and women. All of us—the Masters of No, Wafflers, and Yes-ism people—can benefit from tapping into the Power of No Model.

The decision-points for saying *no* can serve as filters to know whether to say *yes* or *no*. The Power of No Model provides a solid framework for getting to sound decisions that support you and your ability to live the best life for you to live. Other sets of decision-criteria questions abound, such as decision trees, quality criteria, force-field analysis, and others.

And some civic-service organizations prompt members to think about making decisions based on questions similar to the following:

1. Is saying *no* the most kind thing to say? Think about the time you said "no, you look fine" and the person ended up embarrassed.

2. Is saying *no* the most fair thing to say? Think about the time you said *yes* to one child and *no* to another.

3. Is saying *no* an accurate and honest response? Consider the time someone at work was told "no, your work is fine" and ended up getting fired.

4. By saying *no*, are you acting for the highest good of all concerned? Consider whether your saying *no* will be for the best for you, and for others. The act of saying *no* is a form of protection. Invoke and use the word *no* wisely and with careful attention to what the potential results of saying *no* will be.

## POWER PRACTICE: PROTECTING YOUR NO

Next time you decide to say *no*, protect yourself. Protect your delivery of the word *no* by asking yourself these questions.

1. What's my goal in saying *no*? In other words, what do you want to accomplish by saying *no*?

2. How will my saying *no* be heard? As a *yes*? As a *maybe*? As a *no*?

3. In that case, what words will be the best to use?

4. What are the potential responses to the way you'll say *no*?

5. Where will saying *no* get you? How will you go forward?

## THE BOTTOM LINE

The words *no* and *yes* are both important words. When you rely on only *yes* or only *no*, your decision-making stops. Routine answering takes over, causing you to be a Yes-ism person or a Waffler. The Power of No Model questions can help you, or a group, get to the best possible answer for moving forward.

## POWER SUMMARY

1. Use the Power of No Model to define the Purpose, Options, When, Emotional Ties, and Rights and Responsibilities whenever a decision is needed.

2. Be decisive.

## CHAPTER 3

# No *and Self-Protection*

Time, Resources, Self

**POWER PREVIEW POINTS**

1. Priority Decision Grid.

2. Self-defense and the Power of No.

3. Protect your assets with the word *no*.

"I can't say *no*," said Susan, who came to a time management workshop.

"We can all say *no*. And saying *no* is needed if you want to protect your time," said Jana, the workshop leader.

"I can't say *no* at work or at home. There is too much to be done," said Susan.

"You can say *no*. So, what you are saying is that you don't like the consequences of saying *no*," said Jana.

"No," said Susan, from a body with burdened shoulders and anxious eyes. "No. I can't say *no*!"

## SAY *NO*

This chapter stands on the premise that "if you can't say *no*, you can't protect yourself." The need for protection exists in every aspect of life. We want to protect ourselves, our family members, our friends and coworkers. We want to protect our assets, our time, and our money. This chapter talks about—and provides Power Practices for you to record—how you can better protect all these people and things by using the word *no*.

Back to the opening story: Perhaps the denial of Susan's ability to say *no* was indeed the only place she could say *no*. This exchange happened in one of my time management workshops. The class was discussing prioritizing as a strategy for managing time. Using the two continuums of urgency and relevance, as shown in the Priority Decision Grid in Figure 3-1, I was taking the position that there are times to say *yes* and times to say *no*. If a task, an activity, a meeting, or a social engagement does not relate to our goals, desires, and availabilities, then often the best response is a respectfully delivered "no."

## THE PRIORITY DECISION GRID

A word about this Priority Decision Grid—it is a tool for making decisions about where you'll spend your time and how you'll prioritize what you say *yes* to. The primary place to manage your day-to-day life is in the Work-to-Do zone. This is the place in which your focus is on what is important in all parts of your life. That is why it is bigger than the crisis

*Figure 3-1. Priority Decision Grid.*

| Must Be Done Now | Crisis. Do it now! | |
|---|---|---|
| **URGENCY** | | Leave it alone OR leave it for someone else. |
| | Work to be done. | |
| Can Be Rescheduled | | |
| | **Yes Relevant** | **Not Relevant** |
| | **RELEVANCE** | |

zone. The Work-to-Do zone is the one in which we are getting done what needs to be done.

The second place to manage is the Crisis zone. You can't eliminate crisis from your life, so manage through each crisis and move back to the Work-to-Do zone. The place to avoid is the entire Not Relevant zone. If something is not relevant, to you, to your family, to your work, or to your commitments, then why are you spending time on it? Don't. Leave it alone, or leave it for someone else to handle.

At any rate, as I listened and watched Susan, the woman in the opening story, I began to fear for her safety. I wondered to myself, "If she can't say *no* at all, what will happen if she is approached by someone who wants to mug, beat, or rape her? Familiarity with research on what muggers and rapists look for in their victims caused my internal alarms for her safety to sound off. I also found myself reflecting on the personal safety and self-defense class I had recently taken. One of the class teachings focused on the importance of saying *no!*—loudly and forcefully to scare away a would-be attacker. Self-defense experts typically train people to say *no* loudly and firmly, and to mean it. *No* is not negotiable. *No* is a word of warning. *No* is a way of saying, "go away now." *No* is a power tool for protecting your personal space, property, and your body.

## POWER PRACTICE: PRIORITY DECISION GRID

*Scenario 1:* You've been asked to complete a project that doesn't make sense to you, has *no* clear deadline, and doesn't seem to relate to the goals of your business unit.

Where on the decision grid does this fall?

*Scenario 2:* Your child's school nurse has just called to tell you that your child is having a seizure and you're needed at the school.

Where on the decision grid does this fall?

*Scenario 3:* You've just agreed to take on the leadership of a new project. You already have plenty to do.

Where on the decision grid does this fall?

*Answers:*
1. Not Relevant zone   2. Crisis zone   3. Work-to-Do zone

## SELF-DEFENSE

The self-defense-class instructor I worked with was an internationally recognized teacher, educator, professional consultant, and author, Chris Kent. Chris is one of the world's foremost authorities on Jeet Kune Do, the revolutionary martial art and self-help philosophy developed by the legendary Bruce Lee. I talked with Chris at length about how the word *no* relates to self-defense.

During my interviews with Chris, he shared the following information about the importance of *no* when it comes to protecting ourselves:

> From a personal safety standpoint, it's vital to remember that a would-be-attacker is constantly testing the waters and reading signals from potential victims. During this time they are trying to verify whether or not a target is easy prey. Be firm in your resolve. Don't say *NO* and then agree to something. In the case of a potential attacker, it's vital that once you shut them off, you refuse to re-engage them. Ignore their further attempts to talk to you.

Chris, who has studied martial arts for over three decades, goes on to say:

> Self-defense is not about teaching or promoting confrontation or violence. It's about teaching a person how to effectively deal with someone attempting or planning to use violence against them. To me, good self-defense training covers three main elements. The first is *Awareness*. This means being attuned to the environment you are in at any given moment, and involves such things as noticing who and what is around you at all times. Prevention, through good awareness, is much more preferable than cure.
>
> The second element is *Attitude*. The proper mental attitude is that your life and safety is something worth fighting for, and that you have the right to defend yourself. Attitude also helps you to develop awareness of what kind of verbal and nonverbal messages you are sending out via body language and tone of voice.
>
> And the third element is *Preparation*. Preparation involves a combination of setting physical, mental, and verbal boundaries, and developing a working knowledge of basic self-defense skills. Good preparation should also include personal safety education that covers topics such as how criminals choose their victims, understanding

characteristics common to criminals, and tactics and strategies they will use.

In many cases a planned attack is about deception and distraction. And one of the primary keys the criminal assailant will use is dialogue. In this case, it consists of dialogue designed to disarm and distract you, the targeted victim. The dialogue is also meant to get you to lower your awareness and lower your guard. An assailant who seeks to gain your trust is not going to approach you in an overt, hostile manner that would immediately reveal their intentions to you. Rather, they will present an image of being nice so that it is more difficult for you to reject them. Keep in mind that first and foremost it's about control. Used correctly, dialogue can be an effective way to establish some kind of connection and rapport, and manipulate an intended target.

What are some of the language keys you can keep watch for? The first is if a person you don't know uses words such as "we" and "us" in their conversation. For example, while you are pushing your groceries towards your vehicle, a stranger approaches and comments, "Why don't you let me give you a hand? We can do it much faster together." Some will accompany their offers of assistance with promises or guarantees such as, "I'll just give you a hand then be on my way. I promise." Others will use catchy details to give themselves an aura of credibility and become perceived as a person whom you can trust. An example of this might be something like, "I'm always trying to do too many things at the same time myself." And others will use some slight form of insult against you that will compel you to talk to them in order to prove them wrong, such as, "A person like you probably wouldn't want to talk to a person who looks like me." The primary point is that dialogue is used by a criminal to override your doubt about malicious intentions and convince you that he is okay, when in reality, he is a total stranger who is approaching you.

## POWER PRACTICE: IN YOUR DEFENSE

1. How aware are you of your surroundings?

2. What do you do to keep yourself safe?

3. What do you do to help your kids keep themselves safe?

## SELF-DEFENSE PRACTICES IN ACTION

Several years ago, before the days of anthrax-in-the-mail scares, I was hosting a four-hour block of talk-radio shows. One day I received a letter from a listener. It arrived at my post office box in a plain envelope, without a return address and with a hand-written address. In the envelope I found a two-page letter with a return address sticker, a stick of incense, and a cassette tape. I read the letter with interest, and while I didn't feel threatened I did feel like something weird was going on. So, for fun I put the cassette tape into the car tape deck and began listening. After about ten minutes, I stopped listening because I was going into a meeting. Later in the day, I asked a friend for input. I asked her to read the letter and finish listening to the tape with me. Partway through the tape there were threats made to various people and law enforcement officers. At this point, my friend said, "Call one of your cop friends now." At first, I ignored her suggestion. Then, she got more firm and insisted that I call someone to get some ideas about how I should protect myself.

So, I called to file a report on the letter-sender. It turned out, he had been in jail several times, had assaulted police officers, and had a multiple-year history of causing problems in the community. To say that I was alarmed would be an understatement. It had happened: An unstable person had come out of the woodwork and was trying to get into my life. The police immediately made recommendations about how I could protect myself—having an unlisted home phone number, having one of them confront the man and tell him to stop bothering me, to name a few. I said, "*No*, don't contact him. Right now, I'm not a threat to him and I don't want to become a threat. Let's see if there's any more contact, because I'm not a threat to him at this point."

Several months went by without any further contact. Then, one day at the radio station, while I was on the air, I received a phone call from the letter-sender. At first it didn't register. When I realized who it was, I immediately hung up the phone. After that, he made *no* further contact with me. However, it took about a year before I would stop in the grocery store that was convenient for me and near where he lived. Finally, I said to myself, "*No* more, I will not live in fear. This is my life, my community, and it is my right to not live in fear." It was a struggle to get to this new level of confidence. And I believe that part of my progress in reclaiming freedom of activity in my life was taking the self-defense class I mentioned above.

## The Self-Protection Stance

Martial artists, police officers, actors, and athletes all learn that there is a most-effective stance for their respective work. A stance is how you stand or position yourself when interacting with a task or with another person. A stance includes how you hold your body and head, how you find balance, and how you stand. How you gather information and where you look all have an affect on your effectiveness as a performer in each field. Paraphrasing from the professions that require an effective stance, here are six lessons that you can apply as you improve your ability to say *no*.

1. *Lead with your strengths.* Know what your mental and physical strengths for interacting with others really are. Then lead with those strengths. For instance, when saying *no*, your strength may be the ability to say *no* out loud and not care how others feel about your saying *no*. The challenge, in this case, is that your strength can turn you into a target for those people who see your ability to say *no* as rudeness or meanness.

2. *Stay alert.* Know your surroundings. Be careful of getting so focused on who is in front of you that you miss other people and objects entering the picture. Keep your shoulders and head in a position that you can see, hear, and move to adjust to what is happening around you. A *no* overheard by someone without all of the facts may be misunderstood. Protect yourself. As Chris Kent points out, awareness is the first element of protecting yourself.

3. *Keep your distance.* Create a buffer zone that allows you to see what is happening and make adjustments as things change. When saying *no*, the creation of a buffer zone gives you space and time to think things through and to make decisions.

4. *Keep your balance.* If you are down on the ground, you've lost your firm foundation and your ability to stay alert. Find your center of gravity and of balance. When saying *no*, keeping your balance means knowing why you've said *no* and sticking to your response.

5. *Protect your position.* Keep yourself as safe as possible so that you can continue and win the fight, or sink the shot, or make the goal. This is about sticking to your response and being aware of what is happening around you.

6. *Keep your resolve.* Never give up, keep fighting, and performing. Saying *no* is not about fighting. Saying *no* is about being clear about your

goals, stating those goals out loud, working to achieve the goals, and then being gracious enough to thank those who have helped you along the way.

Whatever you do, remember that you have a right to say *no* to all things, people, and experiences. Whether you remember all six of the above points or just one of them is less important than remembering that you can say *no*!

## Self-Defense on the Street

One night on the way to dinner at a restaurant near my office, I had an opportunity to put the above suggestions into practice. A friend and I were walking to the restaurant and were approached by a man asking, "Can you spare a little change?" I shook my head "No," firmly said *no*, and kept on walking without having slowed down. I figured that was the end of the interaction. About ten minutes later, while my friend and I were seated in the restaurant and talking, I saw the same man come into the place we were eating. I was thinking, "He just asked me for money, he's not coming in here to eat." So, I turned to the wait-staff and said "Call the police now." They of course didn't really know what I was saying, so I said firmly three times, and while looking directly at our waitress, "Call the police now please!"

Having finally gotten the waitress to pick up the phone, I turned my attention back to the man who was now one pace from the end of our table. He approached, leaned his legs up against the table, looked at me, and started to speak. Before he could say a word, I had leaned forward on the table, pointed firmly toward the door with my arm, and said loudly and directly, and in a no-room-for-negotiation tone of voice, "My friend and I are having a nice dinner. I'm asking you to leave the restaurant NOW."

It worked. My body language, my tone of voice, my words all worked together and got him to leave the restaurant without having said a word. And I am glad that nothing really dangerous occurred. The police arrived, having found the man on the street, and took my statement. Fortunately, *no* further contact occurred.

I share this story because it was the first time I was confronted in person with a potentially dangerous situation. My training, alarms, and internal voice prepared me to hold my ground and say *no* to the interruption. My body posture and language communicated that *no* so effectively that the intruder left the restaurant without saying a word.

## Tone and Posture Make a Difference

On the subject of body language, self-defense instructor Chris Kent adds:

> From a self-defense perspective, your body position when saying *NO* must communicate to a potential attacker that you mean business and will not be a willing or easy victim. It should not be overtly confrontational and aggressive (unless the situation has already escalated and you are in self-protection mode); however, it should allow you to defend yourself quickly and easily from almost any position. And, it must be integrated with awareness. The bottom line is that you are better off using your gut instinct and approaching another person yourself to ask for assistance than accepting help from someone you feel unsure about. Your chances of being assaulted are much lower.

You can say *no* with your mouth. And you can say *no* with your body language and signals. For instance, red lights, stop signs, and waving red flags tell us to stop. Your body language can do the same thing as these signals do. Your body language can tell someone *"no, stop,"* or it can communicate *"no, I don't like that,"* or state *"no, I'm not going."*

Which of the following postures and body language tools do you use to say *no* to the people with whom you talk?

- Head moving side-to-side indicates *"No."*
- Hand up, palm out, indicates *"No, stop."*
- Crossing your arms can indicate *"No, prove it to me"* or *"No, I'm not moving."*
- Eyes. A mother's glare and slight tilt of the head can say *no* from across the room.
- Eyes. A coworker's or boss' stare can get you to stop talking when in a meeting.

When you keep focused on the issues and depersonalize a conversation that will result in *no*, you are better able to keep your tone of voice from sounding angry, defensive, or blaming. The key to having people hear our "no's" is to say them in a way that is fitting for the situation. Our tone of voice, emotions, and word choice all affect how people hear us say *no*.

Have you noticed that the same word said in a different tone of voice, with a different emphasis, in different situations can take on different meaning? A shouted *no* can cause alarm in others. A quietly spoken *no* can be mistaken for a non-response, or a response lacking in confidence (which is heard as a *maybe*), or can be mistaken for a *yes*. A *no* spoken calmly while looking away from someone may be heard as an embarrassed or guilty *no*. A question mark at the end of the "*no?*" is not an answer or a response, it is another question. A loudly spoken "*No!*" is a firm way to say *no* and to let someone know that you will stand behind your response. When someone says "*noooooooo*," what do you hear?

We can say *no* while shouting, crying, being direct, or firm. We can say *no* apologetically, while smiling, with care, or in anger. Each of these *no*'s means something different and is heard differently by the people around us. Consider the ways a teenager says *no* to friends, compared to saying *no* to you as a parent. A teenager says *no* with different words, different body posture, different attitude, and different eye contact, depending on the audience.

And what about the way you say *no* at work versus the way you say *no* at home? Is it the same? How does your tone of voice change? Consider whether you are calm or agitated in each environment. Consider your levels of patience and firmness in each environment. And consider whether your comfort with saying *no* affects the volume and pitch of your voice when you say the word *no*.

As stand-alone words, there are times when both the word *yes* and the word *no* can tell you where a person grew up. From the Southern states of the United States, you'll recognize the two-syllable "Yeeahss." From the North-central states and from Canada, "Nooo" is a give-away. And from the Western states, a quick and clipped "*No*" is typical. And *no* said sarcastically often means *yes* in American English. So, be aware that the tone of voice you use when saying *yes* or *no* can communicate or confuse your meaning.

### POWER PRACTICE: HOW DO YOU SAY *NO*?

1. When was the fist time you remember hearing the word *no*?
2. What did it sound like? What did it feel like?
3. What tones of voice do you use to say *no*?
4. What do you do with your face, eyes, arms, and body to say *no*?

## LESSONS FROM THE POLICE

In police training, physical presence and body language are a part of using force to manage a situation. The first level of using force to direct or control a situation is to show up in uniform. In other words, a show of personal presence is a potential show of force. In daily life that means showing up in a posture of attention, being alert to when it is appropriate to say *no* and when it is time to move a discussion forward. The second level of force is spoken communication, or verbal commands. This means thinking clearly, speaking articulately, and asking meaningful questions.

Thankfully, the remaining three levels of using force are beyond what we typically need to rely upon when saying *no*. The next three levels are used to deal with active physical resistance (soft-physical techniques), to deal with hostile resistance and bodily attacks (hard-physical techniques), and to respond to the belief that a person is causing, or is likely to cause death or great bodily harm to someone else (deadly force).

Of course you will from time to time—in conversations, discussions, and decision-making sessions—run into active resistance from others as expressed by their tone of voice, body language, or lack of follow-through on agreements and commitments made. If you've worked through the Power of No Model to make a decision, then you can more confidently stick to your *no*'s, even in the face of resistance or challenges that would threaten you or your assets.


## PROTECTING YOUR ASSETS

The ability to say *no* has an effect on all aspects of your safety. Saying *no* is important to your physical safety. Saying *no* is also a safety tool for protecting your assets. Personal assets include your mental and intellectual space, your emotional space, your integrity, your spiritual well-being, and your use of time, money, and talents, and ultimately your health.

Historically the human race has protected itself and said *no* with weapons, wars, words, and symbols. Weapons have been used to say *no* to animals attacking, to human intruders, and to law-breakers. Wars have been used to say *no* to invading countries, to injustice, and to differences in beliefs. Words have been used to say *no* to wars and weapons, to injustice, to bullying, and the word *no* has been used to protect children. And symbols or symbolic objects have been used to say *no* in the form of warding off evil, protecting households, and protecting individuals. Wearing a medical bracelet is a form of protection because it tells people something about you and what not to give you. In both historic and modern life, people have used, and continue to use, painted symbols, talismans, amulets, potions, ritual sayings, rabbit's feet, mezuzahs, crosses, and symbolic eyes in various forms.

In all these cases, the power to protect and the power to say *no* begins with belief. First we have to believe in our right to say *no*. Power then builds upon the faith, hope, and trust that a person has in an object, or an approach for saying *no,* that protection will be provided. Finally, the power to protect and say *no* bursts forth in word and action when a person's confidence and skill combine to externalize the conviction of saying *no* and of protecting one's self, protecting another, or protecting property.

People protect assets in a variety of ways. Protection of assets includes protecting yourself and even saying *no* to things you simply don't want to do. Now, what exactly are our assets? Assets are property, and items of value that are owned, and relationships that you want to keep. People, time, energy, emotions, and relationships are all worthy of protection. The order in which we protect them depends on our life experiences, on the immediate situation, and on what our personal values and goals are.

Only you can determine what is best for you and your situation. I can only offer ideas, approaches, and systems for you to apply in your various life situations. So, here are some stories and approaches for learning to say *no* as a form of protection for your assets.

## YOUR MENTAL AND INTELLECTUAL SPACE

Somewhere in elementary school I read a story about someone who posted a sign in her bedroom about "No dumping." The sign was not a message to keep the room clean. It was a message about not allowing negative, fearful, or sloppy thoughts to enter her thinking. I decided this was a great idea and so posted a "No Dumping" hand-written sign in my bedroom. Well, during the time that the sign was hanging in my bedroom, a visitor from Ireland stayed with my family. One day, she commented on the sign because she was staying in my room and thought perhaps the sign had been hung to tell her to keep the room clean. I was embarrassed. And I explained that the sign had nothing to do with her. It was a reminder to me to be alert and to think clearly.

The words we choose to use show how we are thinking. As a result, saying *no* to the use of certain words is a form of protecting our mental and intellectual space. We use the words "can't" and "I can't" and usually mean "I can do it but I won't," or "I don't want to do it." When we say, "I don't have enough time" we really mean, "I choose to have other priorities."

## POWER PRACTICE: **PROTECTING YOUR MENTAL AND INTELLECTUAL SPACE**

1. How do you protect your mental space?

2. What will you do from now on to protect your mental and intellectual space?

*Potential Answers*

As you read through the potential answers, remember that your life experiences can lead you to different best-answers. Consider each potential answer as an idea starter when you are stuck and as real examples from the lives of others.

1. For instance: Schedule quiet time, even fifteen minutes, during the day to work on projects and solve problems without interruptions. Spend time on activities that refresh your outlook and provide new perspectives.

2. For instance: (Your best answer.)

## YOUR EMOTIONAL SPACE

We all have the desire to be needed and wanted. Being needed fulfills the psychological and emotional need of wanting to be needed. In most cultures, women are more inclined toward the need-to-be-needed outlook on life. So, any request that makes us feel needed is hard to say *no* to.

For people with big hearts, saying *no* to anyone in need feels impossible. The upside is that people are helped and everyone feels good for a while. Eventually big-hearted people often forget to take care of themselves and end up wearing down and burning out. Setting boundaries doesn't mean we shut people out. Setting boundaries means that we have a healthy life balance and that we can feel good more often that we feel bad or tired.

When you say *no*, you are standing up for yourself and setting clear boundaries. You can stand up for yourself by saying *no* to anxiety and pessimism. You can stand up for others by confronting wrongs, injustices, bullying, and lies by saying "*no*, stop, *no* more." Say something or offer ideas that improve a situation. After offering to help make changes, watch what happens. If you are included and want to be included in the changes being made, that's great because things are going your way. If you are ignored or you sense that your ideas and approaches are not wanted or needed, it is time to walk away. It is time to protect yourself, your feelings, and your energy.

A woman shares that while dating a man who had become a U.S. citizen as an adult, she found herself feeling more and more tired. Her positive outlook, possibility thinking, and optimism was always met be his see-the-worst outlook, negative thinking, and pessimism. As much as she loved him, and had pictured that they might someday marry, this woman realized that the emotional bleeding they were doing on each other was actually wearing them both out and keeping them from being happy and energetic. So, with difficulty, they agreed to stop dating. She describes the decision as a protection for both of them.

Speaking of protection, think about the signs you've seen posted on property: "No Trespassing." I've often wondered why we are so accepting of signs on property and so un-accepting of people who say *no* in order to protect their emotional or physical space. Imagine the balance in the world that could exist if we'd all say *no* to being treated poorly by business organizations, volunteer groups, friends, and family members.

## POWER PRACTICE: PROTECTING YOUR EMOTIONAL SPACE

1. How do you protect your emotional space?

2. What will you do from now on to protect your emotional space?

*Answers*

1. For instance: Spend time alone. Spend time with positive friends. Stay away from negative people.

2. For instance: Say *no* to spending time with people who only have sob-stories to tell.

## YOUR PHYSICAL OR PERSONAL SPACE

Cultural attitudes about space affect how close we'll get to other people and how close we'll let them get to us. Individuals raised in the United States tend to want four to six feet of distance between themselves and others. Police officers are trained that anything closer than twenty-one feet is cause for high-alert and readiness. Individuals raised in Europe or Latin America feel comfortable with distances of one to four feet of distance between themselves and others. Arab cultures have different rules of closeness for men, for women, and for men and women together. Asian cultures have rules of physical space and interaction based on age and status.

Protocol specialists and books can help you learn the details. The point here is that we all have a different comfort-zone that defines personal space.

This prompts me to think of a friend's grandson. We were driving with eight-year-old Robert to dinner and talking with him about science and math classes, learning about his life at school. During the conversation, Robert made a comment about not liking people in his "personal space." I asked, "What is your personal space, Robert?" Without hesitation he replied "The whole world." This rings true because as interconnected as we are, in some ways our personal space does extend out into the whole world. Our personal space is affected by what is happening in the whole world because of what the media brings to our doorsteps and—through our TV sets, desktops, and laptops—to our living rooms, family rooms, and bedrooms.

At any rate, while I was pondering the truth of his statement, Robert had thought for a minute and said, "No, just kidding. It's not that big. It's about the size of this car we're in." This comment also made sense. I sat about four feet in front of him and his grandfather sat about five feet in front of him. Then I asked, "So what do you do when someone is in your personal space." He replied, "Well, I have to let people in my space, you're in it right now."

Every day, we each let people into our personal space. We let some people in more than others based on how well we know them, how long we've known them, and whether we are interacting with them in social or business settings, in private or public settings. For instance, while traveling by train in Greece, an American could be identified by his t-shirt commercial, his American English, and by the amount of space he and his family occupied by standing far apart from each other.

You can say *no* to people being in your space in a variety of ways. Business-people who like to hug can be kept out of your hugging-space, by extending your hand toward the approaching hugger and shaking hands. Friends or relatives who like to hug and kiss can be kept from invading your space by exchanging a hug during which you turn your face away and over the other person's shoulder to avoid the kiss. The challenge is that some would find this avoiding behavior offensive. Every culture has an accepted range of comfort that is different. In several European cultures, not exchanging a kiss on the cheek in a greeting is considered rude. Learn to recognize your own comfort zone and that of others. Use words and actions that can protect you.

Protecting your physical space includes being aware of that comfort-zone and safety zone that you can walk through or live in without getting hurt. I remember boys in junior high school throwing rocks at me and another girl when we were walking from our houses to the neighborhood park. She said, "Run!" I said, "No. They can throw those rocks, I'm not afraid. We won't get hurt." And we kept walking. Not a stone hit us because we were outside of the throwing distance of the boys. And I thought, "Aha—saying *no* to being afraid worked. It allowed me to assess the situation, to stand strong, and hold our ground without getting hurt." Again, the key is to assess your physical environments and then use words and actions that protect you.

## POWER PRACTICE: PROTECTING YOUR PERSONAL SPACE

1. What defines your personal space?
2. How do you protect your personal space now?
3. Whom do you let in to your personal space?
4. How will you protect your personal space from now on?

*Answers*

As you read through the potential answers, remember that your life experiences can lead you to different best-answers. Consider each potential answer as an idea starter when you are stuck and as real examples from the lives of others.

1. For instance: Eight feet of distance. My work cubicle. My car. My house.
2. For instance: (Your best answer.)
3. For instance: Family. Friends. Some coworkers.
4. For instance: Meet people in their office for quick conversations. Spend time at home with just family.

## YOUR INTEGRITY

In 1999 I was nominated for and selected as the "Integrity Counts!" Small Business Award recipient, which is an annual recognition program sponsored by the Southwestern Idaho and Eastern Oregon chapter of the Better Business Bureau. The application process caused me to think in concrete terms about the behaviors that define integrity on a daily basis. Behaviors that show integrity include follow-through on what is promised, consistency, honesty, and doing what you say you'll do, when you say you'll do it.

Wafflers undermine their own integrity by being noncommittal.

The Yes-ism person can undermine credibility by not following through on everything committed to. Yet, integrity can be maintained as long as every *yes* is followed-up by the actions promised.

All three say-no approach styles can work and live with integrity. Protect your integrity and your ability to follow through by knowing why you've said *yes* to requests and why you've said *no*.

## POWER PRACTICE: PROTECTING YOUR INTEGRITY

1. What are you doing to stay true to yourself?

2. What are you doing to deliver on your promises and commitments?

3. How do you protect your integrity?

*Answers*

1. For instance: Being honest when I don't want to do something. Speaking up when I do want to do something that someone else is trying to talk me out of doing.

2. For instance: Following through, protecting time to get things done.

3. For instance: Always tell the truth. Make my decisions and my answers as clear as possible.

## YOUR SPIRITUAL WELL-BEING

Living in a state of fear or emotional exhaustion prevents living in a state of spiritual well-being. Spiritual well-being is a state of being in which you live life with time and attention given to the things, activities, and people that feed your soul, that protect your values and beliefs, and that make you feel connected to the world.

Saying *no* to activities and people that are not in keeping with your values and beliefs is a form of protecting your spiritual well-being. Saying *no* to certain words is a form of protecting your spiritual space. For instance, swearing and saying hateful things can wear down a sense of well-being and erode your sense of safety and protection.

Here's an example of how hateful words affected my spiritual well-being because my selfhood and values from growing up were under-attack. When I was in my mid-twenties, I kept hearing parents talk about the school systems their children were in. The discussion turned to bad-mouthing and being very angry with the public school district I had graduated from. Repeatedly discussions ended up this way.

Several months of these occasional conversations, and my not joining in and yet not saying *no*, began wearing on me. I felt like my values and identity were being attacked. I became angry toward the people beating up the school system that I felt was mine and that had contributed to my being who I was. I began to feel like I was being judged, even though I wasn't. My feelings of frustration led to spiritual dis-ease and gave me a glimpse of what can happen when day after day or year after year, words and threats are spoken: People can end up feeling so threatened that they act out violently. The ability to stand strong, without acting out violently, comes from an inner confidence or a spiritual power that you draw on for strength, protection, and inspiration.

Discover what keeps you spiritually alive and connected to your values and the world. Surround yourself with people who support you rather than tear you down. Seek out people and environments that give you time to think, make decisions, and to reflect. Create your own traditions for staying balanced and spiritually healthy.

## POWER PRACTICE: PROTECTING YOUR SPIRITUAL WELL-BEING

1. What life-changing experiences around protecting yourself have you had?

2. What happened? What did you do?

3. What would you do differently now, with the life experience you now have?

*Answers*

1. (Your best answer.)

2. (Your best answer.)

3. For instance: Listen more. Trust myself more. Stay away from people who bring me down, rather than building me up.

## YOUR USE OF TIME

"I don't have enough time," you say. Why is that? Have you said *yes* to too much? When we give away so much of our time that nothing is left for us we tend to grow tired, resentful, and even unhealthy.

I choose to serve on only three to five volunteer boards or committees at any given time. So, when I've hit my personal limit, I can say, "My time is already spoken for with the organizations I'm now volunteering for," and I do not feel badly about turning down another good cause. Several years ago I was at just such a time-limit dilemma. I was approached by the secretary of a volunteer professional association with an inquiry as to whether I'd be willing to run for a board position. Without thinking about how my response would sound and because I was responding from the standpoint of knowing my limits I said *no.* That was it—*no.*

As I watched the reaction on the secretary's face, I realized that I had unsettled him by my abruptness. "I'm sorry," I said. "I've said *no* because I've already reached my commitment load for this year. I am willing to serve on the board in the future." This was the truth and it eased the situation a bit. The secretary then surprised me when he said, "I sure admire your ability to say *no.* I wish I could say *no* more effectively."

Sometimes our being clear about when and why we need to say *no* helps others become more clear about their need and ability to say *no* in order to protect their time, their talents, and their goals.

Cindy, a working mom, shares an example of planning and protecting time, "I use *no* in my personal life as a way to protect time and energy. As I get older, I find that I need to budget and allow for down time. I rarely plan back-to-back evening activities, or attend events that will last past 9 P.M."

Life is a constant battle of juggling time, activities, and responsibilities. Using "no" is a very effective way to protect oneself from getting trapped by trying to please everyone, and yet not pleasing anyone (including yourself).

In the workplace, protection of time ranges from not having to listen to other people's conversations over the cubicle walls to managing meetings. Revisit the Priority Decision Grid at the beginning of this chapter. Use the Grid as a decision tool for deciding how to best protect your time.

Another angle on using *no* in the workplace is found in the sales cycle. Take for instance the story of the salesperson who focused on identifying all of the people who could say *yes* to a proposal. The sales process and proposal were adapted to their needs and questions. Everything seemed in order and ready for the contract to be signed. After the final presentation was made to the buying committee, the committee made its recommendation to the CFO, who was the person who actually had the power to say *yes* or *no* to the deal. And the CFO said *no*.

What lesson was learned? Find out who the people are that can say *yes* and say *no* to a deal, a project, or a purchase. Meet the information and emotional needs of the *yes-* and the *no*-people.

Time can be used, invested, or consumed by activities, conversations, people, and by the way we think. Bill, a forty-something-year-old from the Pacific Northwest, shared this story:

> Recently I found my answering machine filled with messages from a person I hadn't heard from in over a year. Messages were left in the middle of the day. I was awakened in the middle of the night. And I was frustrated. Finally, I determined that just as we pay for the real estate we live in and do business in, so too should people compensate us fairly for the time they take up in our day. When the compensation or exchange of value is not fair, they should be asked to vacate the space—in this case the mental space and the time—that they are consuming. So, I called the person and said that "the friendship is not working and don't interrupt me any more."

Bill's approach was very direct, an approach that might not work for you. You may feel more comfortable with a more conversational approach. The key is that he recognized an abuse of his time and he said "*no* more." You too can recognize the abuses of your time and say "*no* more."

## POWER PRACTICE: **PROTECTING YOUR TIME**

1. What would you like to have more time to do?

2. What do you need to say *no* to in order to have more time to do this?

3. How will you use the Priority Decision Grid to make better decisions?

*Answers*

1. (Your best answer.)

2. For instance: Commitments that don't make you happy, or don't help you meet your goals. Taking on so many projects that you feel burdened or tired all of the time.

3. For instance: Recognize the Not Relevant category items more quickly. Not everything that presents itself as a Crisis really is a crisis. Better schedule Work-to-Do so that the crisis doesn't occur.

## YOUR USE OF MONEY

Say *no* to carrying bad debt. Financial planners tell us that bad debt is anything that doesn't have the potential to gain value or add value to our lives. So, credit card debt on things we eat up, or use up and throw away, is bad debt. Good debt includes things like the first mortgage on our house or an investment in an education. In theory, it is easy and makes sense to say *no* to debt. Yet, as suggested in Chapter 1, our yes-economy in the United States also has made us a nation of high personal debt. I recall a decade ago being called un-American by an insurance agent who learned that I had *no* debt other than my house payment.

Consider the example of Mediterranean countries where even houses are paid for on a cash basis and built only as the cash is available for work to be done. Also, consider saying *no* to impulse purchases. Super-sizing, last-minute shopping, grocery shopping when hungry, and feeling moody or emotional can leave us open to making impulse purchases.

Money management and wealth creation specialists also tell us to say *no* to impulse purchases and to purchases not based on research. Something we already know, yet often fail to apply with our spending habits. And of course, our spending habits influence our saving and investing habits. Consider how you can say *no* more often to protect your money and financial situation.

## POWER PRACTICE: PROTECTING YOUR MONEY

1. Add up what you've spent in the last three days on impulse purchases. How much did you spend?

2. Now consider how you can better protect yourself from making impulse purchases. What will you begin doing differently? What can you say *no* to?

3. What are you saving today so that you'll have money when you are ready to retire?

*Answers*

1. (Your best answer.)

2. For instance: You can say *no* to grocery shopping when you are hungry. Say *no* to check-out stand items. Ask yourself, "Do I really need this?" Ask, "Can I live without it?"

3. (Your best answer.)

## YOUR HEALTH

Study after study shows that our physical, emotional, and spiritual well-being can have an impact on our health. As a result, what we say *yes* or *no* to in our lives can also affect our health. The food we eat, the amount of sleep and exercise we get, and the way we spend our day can all add up to good, or poor health. Tens of thousands of books, resources, healers, doctors, and practitioners exist to guide us in protecting our health. What are you doing to protect your health? What can you say *no* to in order to better protect your health?

## POWER PRACTICE: PROTECTING YOUR HEALTH

1. What are you doing to stay fit?

2. What are you doing to improve your health?

3. Who can work with you on your quest to lead a healthy life?

*Answers*

1. For instance: Walking. Exercising. Eating right. Getting enough sleep.

2. (Your best answer.)

3. For instance: Your doctor, family member(s), friends.

## THE BOTTOM LINE

With every thought and moment-by-moment action, you are making choices and acting on those choices. You can commit to so much that you end up giving too much away and end up giving yourself away without meaning to. Like the story of Susan at the opening of this chapter, you can leave yourself open to harm by believing that you cannot say *no*. What are you choosing?

Saying *no* is an act of protection. Saying *no* is also an act of freedom and an act of justice. More on these in the next chapter.

## POWER SUMMARY

1. Use the word *no* as a protection tool.

2. Use the Priority Decision Grid to make good decisions about how you'll spend your time.

3. Determine what your personal space is and learn to protect it.

4. Work on your Master of No skills. Complete the Power Practices in this chapter to refine your ability to recognize when to say *no*.

**CHAPTER 4**

# The Ethics and Consequences of No

**POWER PREVIEW POINTS**

1. *No* as an act of freedom.

2. Your ethical basis for saying *no*.

3. The Power of No Consequences.

4. Begin your Policy of No.

Oh, for a world where *no* means *no* and *yes* means *yes*. And a world where *maybe* means you'll say *yes* if I can sway you, or you'll say *no* if I can't convince you. Every culture has different meaning attached to the word *no*. This book is written from a cultural perspective in which the word *no* has been abused with "Just Say No" campaigns that weren't reality-based for the intended users. Ours is a culture in which we have been conditioned to say *yes* in order to remain seen as a loving parent or as a team player, and one in which we believe saying *yes* can keep us safe from a larger, more forceful entity.

## AN ACT OF FREEDOM AND JUSTICE

Saying *no* is an act of freedom and of justice. In support of this, David Gill, ethics writer and consultant based in Berkeley, California, writes:

We need boundaries to preserve our own selfhood in a healthy way. There must be a place in our lives for un-invaded privacy so that we can maintain mental and spiritual health. *No* is a part of establishing boundaries. *No* is also the original and primordial act of freedom. *Yes* submits to requests and questions. Without *yes* there can be *no* community, *no* teamwork; without saying *no* there can be *no* individuality. Without individuality, community is flat, uninteresting, and dull.

To have a community, rules and principles for behavior must be in place. Rules and principles guide us on what to say *yes* to and what to say *no* to. For instance, writes Gill, "driving restrictions such as one-way streets are precisely what allows traffic to circulate."

Sometimes saying *no* is based on a rule, restriction, principle, or regulation. Sometimes *no* is an instinctive response. Other times, saying *no* is a reasoned-through, logical, and comfortable response. Saying *no* is not always easy and sometimes saying *no* takes courage. Standing up for your personal values and ideals can be scary, threatening, and even physically dangerous. For instance, saying *no* to interruptions is about protecting time and your freedom to do what you want and need to do. Saying *no* to the things not in line with your values keeps you in your integrity.

Being able to say *no* is also about freedom. During an interview of actor Tom Hanks by Paul Fischer for *www.darkhorizons.com* about the film, *Catch Me If You Can*, Hanks shared his insights on the power of *no* as a word of freedom. Hanks said, "Once I got to the point where I said, 'You know, I don't want to do this,' then that was a hugely liberating moment—where an actor can take one's career in one's own hands. You can call it the power of *no*." Being able to say *no* when we understand that the consequences won't hurt us is indeed a moment of liberation. Being able to say *no* and living with the consequences of saying *no* is also a moment of freedom.

Consider some of the historical figures who have stood, sat, or stopped eating on moral grounds in order to say *no* to a government, or to a way of living. In the first three decades of the 1900s, Mahatma Gandhi repeatedly took a stand and presented the case for Indian independence; eventually he stopped eating in protest to say to England, "India is not yours and we want our country back." In 1989, students in China rallied and protested in Tiananmen Square in support of democracy. They were saying *no* to the way things had been in China since 1949.

During the 1860s, the Civil War was fought in the United States over the moral question of slavery. The "No, it's not right to have slaves" side won the war. On January 1, 1863, President Abraham Lincoln signed the Emancipation Proclamation, making slavery illegal.

After a century or more of fighting for the right to vote, women spread a message that said, "No more of just *men* voting, enough. We deserve the right to vote too." Finally, in 1919 and 1920, women in the United States were given the right to vote when the 19th Amendment to the U.S. Constitution passed. Throughout history, individuals and groups have said *no* to the way things are, and have acted alone or have banded together to bring about a change that is for the betterment of humanity.

"If you want peace, work for justice." Perhaps you've seen this bumper sticker too. This statement says that if you want peace, there are things to say *yes* to and things to say *no* to. Justice is about rights and wrongs—and as such requires recognizing what is right to say *yes* to and what is right to say *no* to. Regular application of the Power of *No* Model can help.

We can and must say *no* in better ways to protect ourselves, our children, and others around the world. We stand at the doorway of opportunity. Walking through the door, we can learn to say *no* in a manner that works for the highest good of ourselves, our communities, our countries, and our world as a whole.

## THE RESPONSIBILITY TO SAY *NO*

For everyone, there is a moral and ethical responsibility to say *no* when appropriate. This responsibility applies to family, work, community, state, and federal decision-making situations. When we fail to say *no* in our families, unruly children grow up, feelings get badly hurt, and sometimes physical harm occurs. When we fail to say *no* in our workplaces, harassment happens, embezzlement and faulty accounting occur, shareholders and employees are let down, and sometimes a company goes bankrupt. When we fail to say *no* in our communities, crime rates and vandalism rise.

There is a need for and a demand for saying *no*. Yet, even with the need and demand for *no*, there are consequences of saying *no*. The positive consequences can be that you protect yourself, others, your time, or your assets. The negative consequences can be that you alienate or offend others, that you miss out on positive experiences, or that others begin to see you as a pessimist who is unwilling to participate in anything. And the neutral consequences of saying *no* can be that nothing especially good or bad happens.

Throughout our lives we've had other people say *no* to us. Some internalize the *no*'s as permanent and non-negotiable. Some ignore the *no*'s and forge ahead with life. Most live in the middle, sometimes accepting *no*, and sometimes rejecting *no*. When it comes to your ability to say *no* to others, you are influenced by your own values, what you hold to be true, and what you believe to be important. Sometimes the values of others also affect the way you make decisions. What you have as a vision for your life experience can also guide to what you'll say *yes* and to what you'll say *no*. Waffling or indecision can come from a lack of clarity about what is important to you, what you value, or want to see happen in your life.

## POWER PRACTICE: DEFINING YOUR ETHICAL BASIS FOR SAYING *NO*

1. What are the principles, values, and rules that you use to guide your decisions?

2. Where did you learn them?

3. Why are they still important to you?

4. Because you are reading this book, there are probably some additional values that you can now add to the list you started in number one above. For instance, what rules for saying *no* would you add?

## HOLD ACCOUNTABLE

Consider this story from Brenda, a college instructor and consultant:

> While collecting papers for the first assignment of the undergraduate class I teach, one of the students was obvious in his efforts to complete the assignment. The student was hurriedly writing answers on his paper as I collected the completed assignment. It had been clear the typewritten assignments were due at the beginning of class. He sheepishly scribbled his name on the top of the paper and gave it to me. Without a word I accepted his paper. The next week when the papers were returned, the student, looking at his underwhelming grade began to complain about how tough the grading had been since he did turn in his assignment. While his teammates watched knowing his work standards were a bit lax, he watched for my response. It was at this moment I smiled at the student and looked at

him directly and said, "Just own it." The other students laughed and the student only blushed. He did not give his argument a second thought. The result of saying *no* to the sloppy work is that this student became disciplined in doing his work on time while meeting standard requirements and successfully completed the course.

## CONSEQUENCES

The student made the choice to turn in sloppy work. The teacher chose to hold him accountable. The student's consequence was a poor grade. And the student chose to become disciplined, or risk the consequence of failing the class.

We each always have a choice. When you don't like the consequences of our choices, you find yourself saying, "I can't," or, "I'll get back to you," or other waffling phrases that you believe will let you off the hook from whatever you've been asked. You always have a choice. When the consequences of a choice seem positive, the tendency is to pursue the choice or option. When the consequences of a choice seem negative, the tendency is to avoid the choice or to not pursue an option at all.

Take this story from thirty-four-year-old Juanita. She was unhappy in her ten-year marriage that from the outside seemed perfect, a nice guy, a paid-for house and cars, no debt, no kids, and comfort and fun times. She shares the story in hindsight:

I was unhappy with my husband. I couldn't exactly put into words why. I just knew that every day I felt weak, like I was drowning. It didn't make sense, since I had what seemed like a perfect life. But my emotions were eating me up. So, I said to my husband, "This isn't working. We are two good people living together like roommates. What can we do to make a marriage, to create a more meaningful relationship?" He wasn't sure. And every idea I came up with didn't seem to work for us. We went to counseling together and on our own. We talked to friends who'd been married more than twenty years. We cried, and talked, and prayed, and talked, and cried some more. After ten months, we ended up getting divorced. Looking back, I realize that I was so tired that I didn't have the energy to see where else we could go with the relationship. I also realize that even though I didn't start the relationship-review conversation with a picture of divorce in mind, I also didn't have a clear vision of where I did want the discussion to lead. I had prepared for the consequence of divorce more than for the consequence of staying together, even though staying married forever to the same man is what I thought I wanted.

Juanita's story points out that the exploration of consequences can take time, can be challenging, and even tiring. Juanita shared that while the exploration process was tiring, she feels good about the outcome because she knows that options and consequences were explored before making a final decision about the divorce. The key to any decision process is to stay in conversation until you have enough information to make a clear decision based on the Power of No Model questions and on the consideration of consequences.

Here's another story that could be you, or me, or someone we know. A woman, Susan, and one of her male neighbors, Joe, realized that they had been taking another neighbor, Esther, to the store on a fairly regular basis when Esther's husband was not available to do so. During their conversation, Susan and Joe discovered that Esther was consistently purchasing alcohol and that they were supporting her in an alcohol-abuse situation. Coming to terms with how to say *no* turned out to be a challenge. Wanting to be helpful, and neighborly meant saying, "Yes, I'll be happy to take you to the store." Being concerned about supporting a destructive habit, saying *no* felt like the best response.

So, Susan says she struggled with whether to avoid the neighbor, to confront the neighbor and risk being wrong and loosing a friendship, or to find the courage to be honest about her concern, and see where a heart-to-heart conversation would lead. Susan applied the Power of No questions in this way:

- **P**urpose. What is my purpose in wanting to help Esther? Susan's answer: To help Esther deal with her problem and to protect the community.

- **O**ptions. What options do I have? Susan chose to talk to Joe about what they might do together to help Esther and to protect themselves and the community.

- **W**hen. As soon as Susan discovered that Joe was also experiencing the same things with Esther's shopping trips, Susan was ready to address the problem. She knew that the timing to talk with Esther had to be in the next few days so that everyone's safety and time could be protected.

- **E**motions. Susan's concern for her neighbor prompted her to take action.

- **R**ights and Responsibilities. Susan realized that her responsibility to care for Esther's well-being and the safety of the neighborhood outweighed her concerns about having Esther potentially being angry.

In the end, Susan and Joe talked with Esther, and with William, her husband. William had not been aware of the problem and was grateful for the discussion. He pursued help for Esther and his family. So Susan's application of the Power of No Model helped her, Esther and William and their family.

Have you faced a dilemma like this, a situation that would have benefited from having the Power of No Model applied? For instance, the *Purpose* of confronting the neighbor might be to help her, or to protect others. The *Options* that Susan felt she had were listed above—avoid, confront, or have a conversation. Whatever option she selected would influence *When* things would happen—when the conversation would happen and when the driving activity would change. The *Emotions* of concern, fear, and courage were involved. And the concern fed into a consideration of the Susan's *Rights and Responsibilities* to herself, to her neighbor, and the neighborhood. Also, Susan had considered some of the consequences of saying, "No more, we need to talk about this." The potential consequences included losing a friendship, protecting someone, and protecting the community.

## THE POWER OF NO CONSEQUENCES

The Power of No Consequences consideration is made of up three questions.

1. What are the positive consequences of making this decision?

2. What are the negative consequences of making this decision?

3. What are the neutral consequences of making this decision?

Your responses to these three questions can guide you in both making a decision, and in choosing behaviors and actions that will help you to follow through on your decision.

The consequences of saying *no* can be explored through the Power of No Consequences questions and through the creation of a Policy of No that can help you determine what you'll say *no* to. The Power of No Consequences prompts thinking through the positive, negative, or neutral consequences of saying *no*. Of course, the same things can be considered when saying *yes*. Whatever your response is after using The Power of No Model, you are most protected when you also consider the potential consequences of your response.

Consequences range from positive to negative. The degrees of positive and negative create a spectrum of potential consequences that you may appreciate or despise, that you may feel comfortable or uncomfortable with, or that may cause you to feel safe or at risk. Positive consequences from making decisions can include protecting your time, self, money, children, property, and other people. Positive consequences can also include safety, job promotion, career opportunities, improved relationships, and problem resolution. Negative consequences can include missing out on exciting opportunities, wearing yourself out, burning out, losing perspective on what really matters, failing to protect yourself, and even endangering yourself or others. Neutral consequences are neither good nor bad, they are things that don't hurt and don't necessarily help get things done.

There are upsides, or positive results, and consequences of saying *no*—you protect yourself or others and you communicate who you are, and what you'll stand for. There are of course downsides or negatives of saying *no* as well—you can alienate yourself from others. And there are some neutral consequences of saying *no*—for instance, others may agree with your position, so *no* questions are asked and *no* challenges are made to your choice.

Sometimes, you take time to consider the consequences of your decisions. Other times, you react and make a decision so quickly that you haven't even considered the consequences. Still other times, you say *no* because you've already made a decision that is now a habit, so you don't have to think an issue through again. Thinking through the potential consequences of a decision can help you make decisions that you can stick to and follow through on. Each time a decision is made, it helps to consider the potential positive, negative, and neutral consequences of that decision.

## POWER PRACTICE: THE POWER OF NO CONSEQUENCES

Consider the consequences of the following say-no statements. Record what you believe the potential consequences could be. The first one is completed to help you get started. For ways to consider consequences, see the potential answers listed at the end of the practice.

*Sample*

> 1. *No to the majority of requests you receive.*
>    *Positive*: You protect your time, or your money. You are able to get done what you've committed to and still have time to do other things.
>    *Negative*: People see you as unwilling to participate in their projects, or see you as a control-oriented person, or as a pessimist. You may not be able to get done what you've committed to because other people feel that you don't help them out, so they don't help you out either.
>    *Neutral*: Nobody seems to feel alienated from you. You are able to get done what you've committed to. Nothing particularly good or bad happens.

2. *No to your boss when a new project demand is made of you. "I want you to take this on."*
   *Positive*:
   *Negative*:
   *Neutral*:

3. *No to your spouse when a yes answer was wanted.*
   *Positive*:
   *Negative*:
   *Neutral*:

4. *No to your kids when a yes was wanted.*
   *Positive*:
   *Negative*:
   *Neutral*:

5. *No to a friend who wants to talk to you about a problem you've heard about before.*
   *Positive*:
   *Negative*:
   *Neutral*:

6. *No to a coworker who asked you for help.*
   *Positive*:
   *Negative*:
   *Neutral*:

7. *No to a customer request that is realistic and easy to complete, yet one that is not profitable for the company to say yes to.*
   *Positive*:

*Negative*:
*Neutral*:

8. *No* to a customer request that your company is unable to deliver on.
   *Positive*:
   *Negative*:
   *Neutral*:

9. *No* to an employee request for increased benefits.
   *Positive*:
   *Negative*:
   *Neutral*:

10. *No* to yourself when you really want to do something new.
    *Positive*:
    *Negative*:
    *Neutral*:

*Practice Answers*

2. *No* to your boss when a new project demand is made of you. "I want you to take this on."
   *Positive*: You get done what was already on your to do list. Your workload stays manageable.
   *Negative*: Your boss is unhappy with you. Your performance review ends up with low ratings. Your boss stops asking you to take things on. You could lose your job. You do lose your job.
   *Neutral*: Your boss is understanding and asks someone else to take on the new project. *No* harm is done, your relationships and standing at work are still in place.

3. *No* to your spouse when a *yes* answer was wanted.
   *Positive*: You've protected your position.
   *Negative*: Your spouse gets hurt or angry. A fight follows your response. Or, no fight breaks out, but you hear about your "no" answer three months later.
   *Neutral*: Acceptance of your answer without any hurt feelings on the part of your spouse.

4. *No* to your kids when a *yes* was wanted.
   *Positive*: You've protected your position. You've protected your kids. You've protected the family.
   *Negative*: Your kids get hurt or angry. A fight follows your response.

*Neutral*: The kids accept your answer without picking a fight, and without any hurt feelings.

5. *No* to a friend who wants to talk to you about a problem you've heard about before.
   *Positive*: You've protected your time, your energy, and your emotional space.
   *Negative*: The friend's feelings are hurt. The relationship with your friend is stressed or broken. The friend's problem was more severe than you realized and something bad happens to your friend.
   *Neutral*: Nothing good or bad happens. The friendship stays in place.

6. *No* to a coworker who asked you for help.
   *Positive*: You protect your time.
   *Negative*: You alienate the coworker. A needed project doesn't get done and you're held partially responsible. Your coworker refuses to help you out the next time you want help.
   *Neutral*: Your response is accepted. No harm is done to the relationship. Work moves on.

7. *No* to a customer request that may be realistic to complete.
   *Positive*: You've protected the company from a difficult customer with unrealistic expectations.
   *Negative*: Everyone is angry that you turned away business: your boss, your team, and the customer.
   *Neutral*: Nothing good or bad results. Business goes on as usual.

8. *No* to a customer request that your company is unable to deliver on.
   *Positive*: You've protected the company from a project that could have hurt the company's reputation or its financial standing.
   *Negative*: The customer is upset or angry.
   *Neutral*: No harm is done to any of the relationships involved. You help the customer find another vendor to work with.

9. *No* to an employee request for increased benefits.
   *Positive*: The company budget is protected. The company policies aren't burdened.
   *Negative*: The employee request was legitimate, legally allowed, and now the employee is extremely unhappy about the denial and resigns from the company.
   *Neutral*: You have a conversation that leads to understanding and *no* hard feelings. The employee stays working for the company.

10. *No* to yourself when you really want to do something new.
    *Positive*: Perhaps you protect yourself from doing something really dangerous that you don't yet know how to do.
    *Negative*: You later are frustrated that you didn't try it. You box yourself in by not trying new things. You lose out on joy and fun-factors in your life.
    *Neutral*: You weren't that attached to doing it, so you're okay with your decision and move on.

## ADDITIONAL CONSEQUENCES

Some additional consequences to consider are these:

- If you say *no* today, will you get asked again when you do want to do it?
- Saying *no* every time, to everyone, can cause you to be seen as a pessimist and can make the word *no* meaningless when you say it.
- Saying *no* all of the time can also be the symptom of problems that are related to unhealthy behavior. If someone you know never says *yes*, consider whether counseling or psychiatric help may be needed.

The key to successful decision making is to make the best possible decisions with as much information as possible (the Power of No Model), with the consequences (the Power of No Consequences Model) in mind, and trusted friends, mentors, or family members to talk things through with. As with so many things in life, finding the right balance is the challenge. The "right balance" of saying *yes* and *no* is something only you can determine for yourself.

## POWER PRACTICE: CONSEQUENCES YOU HAVE EXPERIENCED

1. What are some of the consequences that have inspired you to say *yes?*

2. What are some of the consequences that prompt you to say *no?*

3. What do you feel like when you say *no?*

4. What will you feel like when dealing with the consequences of saying *no?* What will you do? (Feel free to write or draw what it looks like.)

5.  What will you feel like when dealing with the consequences of saying *yes*? What will you do? (Feel free to write or draw what it looks like.)

6.  What will you feel like when dealing with the consequences of saying *maybe*? What will you do? (Feel free to write or draw what it looks like.)

7.  Draw a picture of how you feel when you are dealing with the consequences of having said *no* to someone important to you.

8.  Draw a picture of how you feel when you are dealing with the consequences of having said *yes* to a request to someone you work with.

## THE POWER OF NO CONSEQUENCES IN ACTION

When asked for stories about the moral and ethical implications of not saying *no* when appropriate, Darryl, who is from the West Coast, a husband, father, and grandfather, shared the following. Darryl's story shows a consideration of the consequences of decision making and the moral component of investing time in what and in who we say is important to us.

Dilemmas arise when one agrees to things that they should have declined! My personality inclines me always to say *yes* when I can help someone. I was raised to be part of the solution, not part of the problem, wherever I am. I am healthy, and have a strong work ethic. So, I will help! But it isn't just me that will pay if I agree too often. Yes, I can go with less sleep. I can double my efforts and ratchet up the speed. I can skip a workout or ball game, etc. But that is not always the only way these helping efforts get paid for.

Darryl goes on to say:

Sometimes my family and friends pay. Tonight I am speaking to a graduate student group down at the university. I pay with the effort (it is also a *no*-honorarium engagement). Of course I get satisfaction and applause. But my wife, at the end of a hard week of work, is on her own tonight and will go to bed before I get back. I can't pop in and see my grandkids today because I have to get ready for this presentation. And sometimes, those who need my help pay because I have taken on too much. They may not even notice but I will if I am at half-strength or half-prepared. I should have said *no*. I said *yes* and looked like a great guy, but we are all paying for my *yes* decision.

This story shows that many consequences or "paying for experiences" exist for each decision made, as well as for the total set of choices made on any given day.

## POWER PRACTICE: CONSIDERING THE CONSEQUENCES

1. Given all that you've read thus far, in what situation(s) do you want to say *no?*

2. What are the potential consequences of saying *no* in these situations?

3. How will you handle each consequence?

4. Do you still want to say *no?* How will you say *no?*

5. If you decide that *yes* is the best answer, how can you reduce stress for yourself?

6. What decisions have you made that you and others have ended up "paying for?" What happened?

7. From now on, when you make decisions, what will you do differently?

## AN ETHICAL STRATEGY FOR SAYING *NO*

John, a corporate manager of resource conservation, has reflected on his decision-making approach and says "I share with others the trepidation in saying '*no*' to people, especially people I know and deal with regularly." At the same time, John has found a strategy that works for saying *no*. His strategy is full of integrity and holds true to the theme of this chapter about the ethics of saying *no*. John's strategy:

1. I listen fully to their request without providing any inkling of a reply.

2. I tell them I need to assess my present work schedule.

3. I then take that time to truly consider whether I can say "*yes*" or "*no*" in light of other commitments, appointments, etc.

4. By taking this approach, I find it much easier to reply to them, even as soon as within the hour or later that day, without the gut wrenching pressure the request may promote.

5. Consequently, if I can't say *yes* to their request, I say *no* without any of the baggage.

Have you created a decision-making strategy that works for you? The Power of No Model, the consideration of consequences, and the consideration of integrity all contribute to a sound decision-making strategy. Because the word *no* has come to mean disapproval, negation, denial, and rejection, it is easy to take it personally when someone tells us *no*. Americans have undermined the meaning of *no*. Ethicist David Gill suggests that this is "perhaps because children raised in a relatively permissive era learn that their parents' *no* will not be enforced and so as adults they do not view the word *no* as a necessarily decisive response. And perhaps a society of people addicted to approval may be hesitant to say *no*."

In the workplace, because we want to keep our jobs, to be liked, and to be seen as helpful, it is a challenge to make balanced and sound decisions. The challenges may include that your boss, your coworkers, and your employees may not agree with your decision. And the trouble with saying *no* at work is that there may be an assumption that the *no* indicates a refusal to play with the team or to work for the leader. On the other hand, says Gill, "the ability to say *no* could indicate independent judgment and courage, making one a desirable team member." Again, the consequences and opinions of a decision can be positive or negative.

There are moral and ethical implications of not saying *no* when appropriate. Remember Susan's story about her neighbor Esther? Susan's courage and moral strength caused her to take action toward protecting others. Had Susan failed to say *no* to the unhealthy behavior, negative consequences for families and the whole neighborhood would have followed. Failure to say *no* can cause harm when your failure to say *no* puts you out of integrity and causes others to see you as being dishonest.

## POLICY OF NO

Policy of No statements allow you to make a decision once and then when faced with a similar decision, you can refer to your "policy." The Policy of No statements allow you to quickly make a decision and move forward with the more complex decisions of the day.

The principles, values, and rules that you use to guide your decisions

form your Policy of No. Without a clear understanding of what is important to you, it is easy to say *yes* to everything. Without a personal commitment to the things that you will say *no* to without having to think about
a response, you will end up repeatedly spending time on decisions that
could be made once and then serve as your guides. For instance, if you
believe that hurting someone for *no* reason is wrong, then when you are
in a situation that asks you to hurt someone needlessly, you won't have
to think about it and your decision will be *no*.

Another say-*no* decision that you can make once is, "You may not
have anyone stay overnight when we aren't home." Or, "You may not
drive the car without our permission." Or, "You must be home by 10
P.M. or expect to be grounded." For yourself, you might have a guideline
that says, "I don't give more than 10 percent of my time to volunteer
work." Or to a child selling something at your door, your Policy of No
might sound like this: "Do you live in this neighborhood? I only buy
from kids that live here." Guiding statements like these are your Policy
of No statements.

## POWER PRACTICE: YOUR POLICY OF NO

Building on the first Power Practice of this chapter and the above discussion, list your top ten Policy of No statements. Include statements
that protect your safety, your kids' safety, and your well-being on your
job.

1.

2.

3.

4.

5.

6.

7.

8.

9.

10.

11. Now identify your top three Policy of No statements. Some people
have recorded things like:

"I do not buy things unless I have the cash to pay for them."

"I do not want my kids working during junior high school or middle school so that they can concentrate on school."

"I will not use company property for my personal gain."

## AN UNUSUAL FORM OF NO

I've heard several salespeople share that their secret of sales includes allowing for, and even empowering, customers to say *no*. The rationale for encouraging a customer to say *no* includes the building of trust, integrity, and relationship. When someone can say *no* to us and still interact with us in a sales process we are building the relationship. There are times that *no* is the best response for all involved in a sales conversation. Willingness to accept a *no* response demonstrates your respect for the customer's ability to make decisions. Guard your integrity during the sales process. Know what you'll be able to offer to overcome objections and know what signals and what "no" answers will cause you to back away from the sale and wait for a more fitting time or a more fitting customer. Ask yourself whether greed or the best interests of the customer and the situation are being served.

Another unusual and important way of saying *no* is to decide to stop pretending to be someone other than who you are in order to please others. When you internally say, "no more, it's time for me to be me," your behavior changes and guides what you externally say *no* to. Being true to yourself is a form of saying *yes:* "Yes, I'm ready to be me."

### POWER PRACTICE: BEING TRUE TO YOURSELF

1. Who is asking you to be someone you are not?

2. How will you say *yes* to being yourself and *no* to the person you named above?

3. How will you say *yes* to being yourself when you talk yourself into behaving in ways that are not true to who you are?

## MAKING CONNECTIONS

Before this chapter comes to an end, let's connect the Masters of *No*, the Wafflers, and the *Yes*-ism people to the discussion of ethics and integrity.

Each of the three say-no approaches uses different words to communicate a decision. The potential words for saying *no, maybe,* and *yes* are discussed in the next three chapters. Here, let's explore how much respect and integrity each say-*no* approach is potentially demonstrating.

For the most part, a Master of No is being ethical because that is part of the definition of being a Master—"saying *no* when it is appropriate." However, a Master of No can become so dependent on saying *no*, that *no* becomes the Master's only response. When this happens, the ethics of and respect for decision making have slipped and it's time to revisit the Power of No Model to improve the decision-making process again.

Wafflers are constantly avoiding a decision. This continual decision-avoidance is not ethical because it leaves people believing you've said *yes* when you haven't. Wafflers are also being unethical when they don't produce an answer for which someone is waiting, or when someone's life depends on it, or when work is held up waiting for the decision. On the other hand, Wafflers who gather information that leads to a decision are being ethical to their word, "let me do some research and get back to you."

The Yes-ism person lives life believing that all is well: "I'm being helpful" and "I mean well." While these statements may be true, Yes-ism people are typically making false promises because not all of the things they promise actually do get done. False promises are not ethical.

From time to time, we all make a poor decision. Sometimes we can get trapped into self-centered thinking, such as greed, and fail to make the best possible decisions for all concerned. And occasionally we make decisions that are not as full of integrity as we would like. The key is to make the best possible decisions (*yes* or *no*) with the best possible information (using the Power of No Model). Even when we've made the best possible decision at any given time, sometimes things still don't turn out as planned or hoped for. When this happens, recognize what went wrong, what happened after the decision was made, who was involved in causing things to change, and determine what can be done differently next time. Keep yourself from getting distracted and keep moving forward. You made the best possible decision that you could, so keep making the best possible decisions and move forward with your life.

## THE BOTTOM LINE

It is worse to say *yes* and mean *no* than to say *no* in the first place. Saying *no* works when you say *no* based on your values, beliefs, boundaries and Policy of No statements. Being true to yourself is a basis for saying *yes* and *no* to a variety of requests, whether the requests are made by a spouse, a child, a coworker, a friend, or a supervisor.

The bottom line is that ethics are a part of the Power of No Model because ethics are a part of the Rights and Responsibilities discussion. So, know your rights, your company policies, your family policies, be decisive, and follow through.

## POWER SUMMARY

1. Power of No Consequences: Think through the potential positive, negative, and neutral consequences before you make a decision.

2. Policy of No: Complete your list of say-no policies.

3. Ask, "Is my response ethical, honest, fair, considerate, and for the highest good of all concerned?"

## CHAPTER 5

# *Saying* No

You Can Say *No*

## POWER PREVIEW POINTS

1. Learn to say *no*.

2. Words for saying *no*.

3. Discover your say-no personalities.

4. Finish your Policy of No.

The focus of this chapter is learning to say *no* out loud, after choosing the best possible words to say *no*. An internal desire to say *no* doesn't get heard. Speaking out loud is the other half of the say-no process. Many people believe that they are telling someone *no* or even rejecting a person when they are saying *no*. The act of saying *no* is really focused on an issue, process, behavior, action, responsibility, or principle rather than being directed at a person.

## MATCHING THE INTERNAL *NO* TO THE EXTERNAL *NO*

Saying *no* is an internal experience before it is an external experience. First, you think about saying *no*. You talk yourself through why and whether you'll say *no*. You hope you'll say *no* when presented with the opportunity to say it out loud. The intention and desire to say *no* may grow to the point that you feel comfortable saying *no* out loud.

Some people have shared that their internal voice says *no* in these ways. "No, I won't let you hurt me. No, I won't take this any more. No, it does not have to be this way." The challenge is that even when you decide in your mind to say *no*, you don't always end up saying *no* out loud for others to hear you.

Why is that? You create an internal (wanting to say *no*) and external (saying *no* out loud) mismatch for dozens of reasons. You think *no* and say *yes* when you don't want to look bad. You say *yes* after thinking *no* when you want someone to like you. Kids say *yes* when they want to say *no* so that they'll have friends. You say *yes* when you're tired and don't have enough energy to say *no*. And the situations that create a mismatch go on.

Again, the decision to say *no* is both an internal and external experience. Saying *no* is also both a reasoned and an emotional response. Most often you have time to pause and reason through whether saying *no* is the best response. On the thankfully rare occasions that you don't have time to reason through saying *no*, your instincts drive your reactions, and you know that *no* is the right and most safe response. Here's the key. If you feel and know that *no* is the right thing to say, then say *no*. Say *no* when you are feeling danger. Listen to yourself, trust yourself. Don't talk yourself into a *yes*. It is not always necessary to be nice. If you feel threatened, then that's when you urgently want to say *no*.

When you want to say *no* and feel like you can't or won't say *no*, ask yourself why. Is it because you are afraid you will look bad if you say *no*? Is it because you don't want to feel badly about saying *no*? Is it because you're not sure of the consequences? Or, is it because someone else tries to make you feel badly when you do say *no*? Focus on creating a match of what you want and what you'll say out loud.

Consider the following signs, stories and messages about saying *no*.

"No soliciting." That's the sign by a neighbor's front door. How clear are you about what you'll listen to and what you will shut out? The "No Dumping" story told earlier communicates a similar message: "I'm only letting in what I want to listen to and what is healthy for me." These signs tell people what the person who posted them is saying *no* to.

While working my way through college, I held a job as a deli-counter server in a grocery store. One busy lunch hour, a customer on the other side of the counter was pacing, swearing under his breath and yet loudly enough for other customers to hear. He seemed to be angry with the world and was letting everyone know that he was unhappy. The coworker waiting on him had to go to a kitchen refrigerator to get the item he had asked for. While she was away from the counter, his angry behavior began to be directed at her. By this time other customers had grown uncomfortable and were moving away from him. Observing all this, and despite having heard "the customer is always right," I internalized that "this is NOT all right, and I have to say something." So, looking directly over the counter at the customer, I clearly, firmly, and apparently fairly loudly, said, "Sir, she has gone to get the food that you requested. She is working to meet your needs and will be right back with what you want." So, while I didn't say out loud, "No sir, your behavior is not acceptable," the words that I did say out loud made the point that his behavior was not acceptable and he calmed down long enough to be handed his order and leave the deli area.

Then a customer who had been waiting in line and seen his behavior was the next customer I waited on. She said, "Thank you for saying something to him. I can't believe how he was behaving and I didn't know what to say." Proof I thought then—and still think today—of several things. First, customers are not always right, and customers shouldn't have to say *no* to or stand up to each other. Second, as service providers, we get to set the standard for whom we will work with. Third, people notice poor and irritating behavior and typically feel intimidated or afraid to do or say anything, and as a result are happy to cheer or say *thank you* when someone else speaks up.

Finally, this story shows that we can say *no* effectively, clearly, and graciously in order to protect ourselves (me and my coworker behind the deli-counter), others (the other customers standing nearby), our employers (from a customer complaint or worse), and our employer's brand (this was an upscale grocery store known for its attractive décor, fine food, and excellent service).

## POWER PRACTICE: SAYING *NO*, MAKING THE MATCH

1. When have you thought "no, this isn't right" and said *no* to stand up for improved behavior?

2. What did you say?

3. Did anyone express appreciation? Who?

4. How did you feel?

## HEALTHY SELF-TALK

People who clearly set boundaries and protect themselves do so because they are able to match their internal self-talk and externally spoken *no*'s.

Healthy self-talk can help turn an internal *no* into an external *no*. Use any of the following phrases as part of your healthy self-talk.

No, I choose not to be a victim.

No, I always have a choice.

No, I don't like it.

No, I don't like it, and I do understand it.

No, I'm not going to listen to one more obnoxious joke.

No, I'm not going to continue working for less than I am worth.

No, I'm done letting myself get worn down by this person and situation.

## POWER PRACTICE: YOUR SAY-NO SELF-TALK

1. What words do you use now to coach yourself to say *no*?

2. Why do you need to say *no* more effectively?

3. What are your favorite words for saying *no*?

4. What words will you start using to say *no*?

5. Self-talk, reflection: Do the people you speak to understand you? Or do they get confused? (If others are confused when you think you have said *no*, it means that you are not used the word *no* as a complete sentence.)

## HOW YOU WILL SAY *NO*

Saying *no* is a protection, a stand against injustice, and an act of freedom. Masters of No use the word *no* to mean *no*. They understand the consequences of saying *no* and have determined that saying *no* is the best and ethical thing to say.

Visualize yourself saying *no*. If you can't imagine yourself saying *no*, then your ability to say *no* drops to nearly zero. Consider again to whom you would like to say *no*. Picture this person and the situation you are in with this person. Think through the following questions to determine how you will say *no* and mean it.

1. What is motivating you to say *no*?

2. What are you hoping for? Why do you want to say *no*?

3.  What consequences are you prepared to handle?

4.  How are you standing or sitting?

5.  What does your face look like?

6.  What tone of voice are you using?

7.  How will you handle the person's response to your saying *no*?

8.  Look to where you want to be when you say *no*.

9.  Hear how you will say *no*.

Now, say *no* out loud. Right now, say *NO*. If you didn't just find yourself saying *no* out loud and with meaning, here are some questions to help you practice saying *no* out loud and with meaning. Remember, if you can't say *no* when *no* one is listening, how will you confidently say *no* when someone is listening? Respond as quickly as possible to each of the following questions. Say your answers out loud!

1.  Do you want to work 100 hours a week every week?

2.  Do you want to get paid less than you are worth?

3.  Do you want someone to permanently take your kids, so that you'd never see them again?

4.  Do you want to eat until you explode?

5.  Do you want to be involved in a fatal car accident?

## POWER PRACTICE: LEARNING TO SAY *NO* OUT LOUD

*Practice in front of a mirror:*

1.  With your eyes closed and without saying a word out loud, practice saying *no* silently, in your mind. Say *no* to yourself silently five times.

2.  Now, with your eyes open, say *no* five times to yourself.

3.  Next, with your eyes closed, say *no* out loud five times.

4.  Finally, with your eyes open, say *no* out loud five times.

5.  Say *no* out loud in five different tones of voice.

6.  Say *no* out loud with five different facial expressions.

You can also practice saying *no* while commuting—with your eyes open of course. Also study the long list of ways to say *no* in Appendix C for potential words to use when saying *no*. Select words that are comfortable for you to say.

## CREATING *NO* STATEMENTS THAT MEAN *NO*

Just because you mean *no* doesn't mean that others hear you say *no*. Make *no* the first word in your response. Then build a sentence that supports your *no*. Build a sentence that stays *no* and doesn't turn into waffling. When building a *no* statement that means *no*, you want all "yes" answers to the Power of No Model questions that follow:

- **P**urpose: Does the word *no* appear at the start of the sentence?
- **O**ptions: Do you know that there are *no* options and *no* resources to help you get this done?
- **W**hen: Does the sentence state clearly for how long you mean *no*?
- **E**motions: Have you acknowledged how you feel about what you are going to say?
- **R**ights: Have you considered your rights, responsibilities, and potential resources, or the consequences around saying *no*?

If you can't say *yes* to all five questions, you are putting yourself in the maybe-waffler position—a position in which others will think you are not making a decision or that you are saying *yes*.

Here are some more questions to consider and visualize so that you can begin preparing your mind, heart, and body to say *no* when you want to. The Masters of No already know how to do this.

1. What do you want to happen when you say *no*? Picture it.
2. What happens after you've said *no*? Picture this too.
3. How will you relax and have fun saying *no* (without creating pain for someone else)?

Be positive about your ability to say *no*. Focus on what you can do and say *no* to the rest.

There is a time for *yes* and a time for *no*. When you decide *no* is the right, best, most safe, or most ethical answer, then say *no*. Speak out loud the right response for the situation and for you.

## POWER PRACTICE: **PRACTICE SAYING *NO* AGAIN**

Another way to practice saying *no* out loud is to begin saying *no* to people you don't know. It's usually easier to say *no* to people you don't know. So, the next time you're in one of these situations, practice saying *no* to:

1. The friend's dog that jumps on you as you walk through the front door. (For example, most people push the dog away while saying *no, no* in a playful way. A Master of No says, "No. Stay down.")

2. The person selling something at your front door.

3. The receptionist who asks if you'd like to wait on hold.

4. The mall surveyor who asks if you have a minute.

5. The store clerk who wants your telephone number for their marketing department.

6. The waiter who asks if you'd like fries with your meal.

7. The waitress who asks if you'd like dessert.

8. The rental car agent who wants to upgrade you to a bigger car for just ten dollars a day.

9. Answering your cell phone when you are talking to someone face-to-face.

## WORDS FROM THE POWER OF NO SELF-ASSESSMENT

From the Power of No Self-Assessment, you can focus on the words you choose to use when saying *no*. The Masters of No often say *no* in the following ways. The numbers indicate which self-assessment question each statement comes from. These say-no statements are fairly clear. However, they can be made into even more clear messages of *no*.

1. "No." This is a complete sentence and means *no*.
6. "No way." Emotion is attached to these words. There's no room for negotiation.
7. "No, thank you." A clear and gracious way to say *no*.

10. "What part of *no* don't you understand?" This question grows out of frustration and can be confusing to some listeners. A more clear way to say what this means is: No.

13. "My schedule doesn't allow me to take that on at all." The *no* part of this sentence is "take that on at all." Put the *no* up front so that it is clear you are saying *no*. Clearer options are: "No, my schedule doesn't allow me to take that on at all," or, "No, my schedule doesn't allow me to."

16. "I won't do that at all." Again, put the *no* up front so that it is clear you are saying *no*. A more clear option: "*No*, I won't do that."

19. "Stop. Don't do that." Spoken as an immediate form of protection, this is clear on its own.

As pointed out in question 13, put *no* at the beginning of your response. The further into your response you place the word *no*, the greater the chances that your *no* will be lost. And a lost *no* can turn your response into a *maybe* or even a *yes*.

## NO. *NO*. NO! THE WORDS WE USE

The following phrases, once used, have to be followed by your sticking to your word. Otherwise, you negate the word *no* all over again and move immediately to being a Waffler. Read through the list of *no*'s and the related meanings. Highlight the words you will use when you decide to say *no* out loud to someone.

"No." No excuses or explanations, I mean *no*.
"No!" With excitement, you are telling me *no*.
"No!!" With loudness, you are telling me *no*.
"No, thank you." You respect me and my request and you are telling me *no*.
"No, not ever." You are telling me whatever I've asked will never happen.
"No, I can't fit it in." You're telling me that you can't do what I wanted help with.
"N.O." This is often said to children. You are saying *no*.
"No" (shouted). This is a protective *no*.
"No" (firmly). This is a non-negotiable *no*.
"No" (confidently). This is a steady, polite, and non-negotiable *no*.
"No" (like you mean No from the depth of your being). This *no* says

that you care about what I am asking you and that you are saying
*no.*
"No way." You are telling me that my request won't be honored.
"Absolutely not." You are telling me that there are *no* options and
that my request will not be granted.
"Negative." You are or were in the military and are telling me *no.*

The following *no*'s are all ways of saying *no* in order to protect yourself or someone else.

No. Get away from me.
No. Don't touch me.
No. Don't come near me.
No, don't let your dog near me.
No, don't let your cat near me.
No. Just look.
No. Don't get in, it's too hot.
No. Stand back.
No. Leave right now.

Commonly seen signs that say *no* remind us that saying *no* is a valid
and important part of life and of living in a community that is as safe and
manageable as possible. These commonly seen signs are found in a variety
of places: at work, at community locations, on private property, and on
public property. Which of these signs have you seen recently? Which are
hanging in your neighborhood? Which are found at your workplace?
Which are found by pools and at schools?

No soliciting.
No smoking.
No shirt, No shoes, No service.
No running.
No swimming.
No diving.
No fishing.
No trespassing.
No hunting.
No dumping.
No firearms.
No bicycles.
No motorized vehicles.

## Social and Family Situations

The words we choose to say *no* at work are not always the same words we'd use at home. And the same is true in reverse. What works at home doesn't always go over well at work. The following phrases might work for you at home or with friends:

No, that's not in your best interest.
No, that's not in our best interest.
No, I'm not up for a movie.
No, he can't go to the dance.
No, she can't stay out past 10 P.M.
No, I'm too tired.
No, I'm not at my best.
No, we don't need that.
No, we won't have the money for that.
No, I won't buy that for you.
No, put it back.
No. Don't touch.
Enough already. I said *No*.
No. (A May 12, 2003 *Time* magazine article, "A Working Mother's
    Day from A to Z," included for the letter *N*: "No: Useful word.")
No, No. (As spoken to a child.)
No. (As defiantly spoken by your two-year old.)
No. (As defiantly spoken by your thirteen-year old.)
No. (As stated by your nearly legal-age child.)
No, I don't drink alcohol.
No, I don't do drugs.
No, I don't smoke.
No, I don't have sex.
No, I don't have unprotected sex.
No means no.

## HOW PEOPLE SAY *NO*: YOUR SAY-NO PERSONALITY

You say *no* based on your personality, your life experiences, your understanding of the situation and your understanding of the consequences. The Power of No Model helps to define the situation. A consideration of the positive, negative, and neutral consequences may point you in a different direction. And of course, your life experiences are always present, influencing how you respond to people and situations.

Your personality and emotions also affect the way you say *no*. When you are gracious and say *no*, you sound different from when you are angry and say *no*. When you are safe saying *no*, you sound different from when you feel danger. So, when your emotions are in action, your responses sound different. And my responses in the same situations will sound different from yours because we don't have the same life experiences and personalities.

Emotions affect tone of voice and body language, which in turn affect how well others can hear you say *no*. Presence is the attitude, demeanor, vocal tone, body language, and eye contact that you use when you communicate. Each say-no personality has a related say-no presence.

Here's how you can recognize the say-no *personalities*. The say-no personality style is listed first and followed by a brief description and example of how *no* is said by each personality. The say-no *presence* for each say-no personality is also listed.

- *Direct.* You don't add words or make excuses for saying *no*. There's *no* room to negotiate: "No." *Say-no presence*: Someone who says "no" *directly* is seen as firm, confident, loud enough to be heard, and who speaks to the point. A direct say-no presence includes a level tone of voice and direct eye contact.

- *Indirect.* You mean *no*, but your words usually turn you into a waffler: "I don't think I can." Or worse, you say *yes* and then don't follow through because you never intended to. *Say-no presence*: Someone who says "no" *indirectly* is seen as uncomfortable, quiet, not loud enough to be heard, and who provides extra information. An indirect say-no presence sounds and looks like a Waffler to others because of a soft volume, indecisive tone of voice, and a habit of looking away from requesters.

- *Gracious.* You use firm, polite, and gracious words to say *no*. You are considerate and respectful of the request and the requester: "No thank you." *Say-no presence*: Someone who says "no" *graciously* is seen as kind, respectful, confident, loud enough to be heard, and considerate. A gracious say-no presence uses a warm tone of voice.

- *Detailed.* You know why you are saying *no* so you share the details in your response: "No. I'm not committing to another project because the ones I've got are already falling behind." *Say-no presence*: Someone who says "no" from a *detailed* personality is seen as neutral, reasoned, able to back decisions up with details, and loud enough to be heard. A detailed say-no presence uses even tones and energy when speaking.

- *Inspired.* You feel comfortable saying *no* and do so in a way that keeps others from feeling hurt or offended: "Thanks for thinking of me. No, I'm not passionate about that cause, so I won't be participating." *Say-no presence*: Someone who says "no" from an *inspired* personality is seen as comfortable, confident, considerate, relaxed, and loud enough to be heard. An inspired say-no presence uses calm and confident tones of voice.

- *Greedy.* You use *no* as a form of control over other people. When others hear you say *no* they seem to feel offended or hurt. "No. What were you thinking? You know that can't be done that way. No. I'm not going to help you re-do it." *Say-no presence*: Someone who says "no" *greedily* is seen as firm, obnoxious, very loud, scattered, controlling, and sometimes selfish. A greedy say-no presence uses a varied tone of voice and often a raised pitch of voice.

Return to the three skill levels and say-no approaches: Master of No, Waffler, Yes-ism person. As you expand your understanding of the approaches, words, and decision tools, the language introduced in this book will become more easy to remember and more comfortable to apply. The say-no personalities tie to these three self-assessment categories. Here's how:

- The direct, gracious, detailed, and inspired say-no personalities are seen as appropriate Masters of No.
- The greedy say-no personality is seen as an abusive Master of No.
- The indirect say-no personality is seen as a Waffler or Yes-ism person.

## MASTER OF NO PERSONALITIES

Here are some stories from six Masters of No in action and demonstrating their say-no personalities. As you read each story, see whether you can identify the singular or combination say-no personalities in action.

### Anne

Anne, a retired personnel and communications specialist, tells this story of learning to protect her time and say *no*.

> I know as a type A person, that I was always thinking I could fit in one more thing, until I was diagnosed with breast cancer. I finally

had a good reason to say *no*. At that same time, I realized that I always had that power, but I had never used it. We had a manager who once said when he had to say *no* in difficult situations that his people would look at him and expect him to change his mind. Then he would respond, "Which part of *no* don't you understand?" That became a stress-relieving joke with the employees. When one of us would say *no*, we would look at each other and repeat, "Which part of *no* don't you understand?"

As a Master of No and of Directness, Anne concludes that "sometimes you don't even need to have a reason to say *no*. It is your right and your privilege to be able to say *no*. You don't have to make up an excuse. Once you've decided to say *no*, say it, and stick to it."

## Greg

It is usually less challenging to stick to having said *no* when we're clear on our reasons for saying *no* and our Policy of No statements are clearly defined. Here's a story with both clear reasons and policy statements for saying *no*. The Honorable Greg Casey, a former U.S. Senate Sergeant at Arms, shares his story:

> A well known U.S. Senator left the Senate. As a member of the Senate, he got a special license plate (usually displayed in the front window) that allowed members of Congress to park in reserved places at Washington area airports. The rules were that only current members of the Senate had the right to the special plate. So, the call came in requesting that I extend that right to this recently retired and prominent former senator. I said, "The rules don't allow it and I am the primary enforcer of the rules. No." The senator then said, "All your predecessors have." I said, "That isn't my concern. What is my concern is the enforcement of the rules. No plate." Mr. Casey's say-no personality in this case was *direct*.

## Connie

Connie, a magazine editor in Florida, writes, "My partner said that when his children were small, and they wanted to do something he and his wife wanted to forbid, they would say, "I love you very much, but this I cannot let you do." He claimed it worked very well. (Maybe only for the parents.)" Connie's partner has a gracious and direct say-no personality.

Another situation Connie addressed is the dreaded solicitation call.

"When a charity I do not intend to donate to calls, I tell them, 'I respect your cause as a good one, but right now I am putting children, hunger, AIDS, and civil liberties at the top of my list, and your charity is not included.'" Connie's favored say-no personality appears to be gracious and detailed.

Now apply the Power of No Model to Connie's say-no statement for telephone solicitors. The *Purpose* of her saying *no* was to be nice, yet firm, about not donating to the cause. The *Options* Connie listed were the causes she would support "children, hunger, AIDS, and civil liberties." The *When* or time-frame of Connie's options list is an indefinite "for now." The *Emotional Ties* are two-fold. First, Connie expresses that she does "respect your cause as a good one." And second, Connie is clearly attached to the four causes at the "top of my list." And the *Rights and Responsibilities* part of the Power of No Model really rests on the fact that Connie is clear about the causes she will support to contribute back to the community and the world, and can name those causes without having to think about them. In other words, she has established guidelines for who has a right to ask and expect her to give money to their cause.

## Linda

Linda, a communications manager in the paper industry, shares this story of *no-never*:

> I pattern my saying *no* after a segment in my business writing skills workshop that I used to train. I called it "How to say *no* without twisting the knife." The lead in I used was relating a story that a friend of mine told me years ago. He said when he was a freshman in college, and away from home for the first time, he got desperately homesick. He welcomed every letter from his family members, including his little sister who was seven years younger. One day, he was feeling particularly down, but cheered up when he saw a letter from his sister in his mailbox. It said, "Dear Jack. Mr. Happy Toes is dead." Mr. Happy Toes was the beloved family cat.
>
> So, when delivering bad news, or saying *no*, don't use the "Mr. Happy Toes is dead" approach. It's too brutal. What I usually do is tee up the situation with a brief statement that summarizes my current situation (at work, in life, whatever) and start the sentence, "As you may know. . . ." Then I add some information that introduces the complicating factors that precipitate my saying *no* (overextended, timing not right, really not the right person, whatever). Then it's a clean jump to the "no, really sorry, but *no*."

In this story, Linda's say-no personality is a combination of detailed and gracious.

## Marguerite

Marguerite, a former corporate executive, business owner, and business development consultant, says:

> At work I might say, "I cannot approve a raise for you this year, even though you met all of your objectives. We have no money for increases for anyone this year. I have been very pleased with the way you have managed the XYZ contract all year and that is reflected on your performance review. You are a valuable part of our team and I hope you will choose to stay with us."
>
> In this example, Marguerite is using a direct and inspired combination say-no personality. Marguerite goes on to say, "My success in saying *no* varies with the person I am saying it to. One friend, a master of unsolicited input, tends to ignore my gentle *no*'s and continues to forge ahead over my protests. So my *no*'s get shorter and more abrupt until I say, 'Stop right now before you ruin our visit.'" Her final response is direct, bordering on greedy, because of her frustration in the described situation and because she wants to regain control of and balance in "the visit."

## Bernard

Bernard, a corporate executive and former board member, shared this story:

> I have said *no* to the Board about continuing my role as a director, board member, after November 1. It has been seven years and it is time to say "no more." I have had to take a hard look at this and have decided that I am ineffective and spinning my wheels. So, I am saying *yes* to my core projects and core business. Believe me, this *no* was neither easy to say, nor to hear.

Bernard's say-no personality is both detailed and direct. He has said why he is saying *no* and has put a clear time frame on when his *no* takes effect.

## POWER PRACTICE: **YOUR SAY-NO PERSONALITIES**

What say-no personality do you tend to use the most? Is it effective for you? Are you sure? The say-no personalities can be used in combination to say what you mean and to protect your relationships with the people you say *no* to.

1.  What is your say-no personality?

2.  What is your boss's say-no personality?

3.  How will you use the Power of No Model to improve the effectiveness of your discussions and problem solving?

4.  What is your spouse's say-no personality?

5.  How can you better navigate conversations at home?

6.  What is your best friend's say-no personality?

7.  How can the two of you support each other as you become a Masters of No?

## POWER PRACTICE: **YOUR SAY-NO PRESENCE**

The physical presence of saying *no* has an effect on whether people will take you seriously. How you stand, sit, look, speak, and gesture will influence people when you say *no*.

1.  How do you look now when you say *no*?

2.  What can you do to physically communicate that you are saying *no* and mean it?

3.  What tone of voice will you use to be serious and nonthreatening about saying *no*?

4.  What tone of voice will you use to be serious and threatening about saying *no* in these situations?

    *No* to protect your safety, or that of a child:
    *No* to meetings:
    *No* to projects:
    *No* to volunteering:

*No* to unmanaged business growth:

*No* to invitations:

5. What is your typical say-no presence?

## PERCEPTIONS ABOUT SAY-NO PERSONALITIES

Where do you recognize yourself using each say-no personality? This is important to reflect on because each say-no personality is seen very differently. Here's how each say-no personality tends to be seen by others: the positive, the negative and the neutral.

- *Direct*
  Positive Perceptions: "You're decisive."
  Negative Perceptions: "You're rude." Or, "I'm not sure you heard me out before making your decision."
  Neutral Perceptions: "You're clear, I'm clear."

- *Indirect*
  Positive Perceptions: "You're nice."
  Negative Perceptions: "You haven't given me an answer, I don't trust you to give me one." Or, "Why are you always making excuses?"
  Neutral Perceptions: "I feel, or see, things the same way you do."

- *Gracious*
  Positive Perceptions: "You're nice, kind, and considerate."
  Negative Perceptions: "You're overly nice and I'm not sure I trust you."
  Neutral Perceptions: "I appreciate your response."

- *Detailed*
  Positive Perceptions: "I know why you made your decision."
  Negative Perceptions: "You've buried me with details."
  Neutral Perceptions: "I would have shared similar information."

- *Inspired*
  Positive Perceptions: "I almost feel good hearing you say *no*."
  Negative Perceptions: "Why are you always so happy and upbeat?"
  Neutral Perceptions: "Thanks for the conversation and the options."

- *Greedy*
  Positive Perceptions: none.
  Negative Perceptions: "You're not nice." Or, "You're a jerk." Or, "You are offending me."
  Neutral Perceptions: "I feel or see things the same way you do."

# SAYING *NO* WITH THE SAY-NO PERSONALITIES

Here are some no's that can be heard in the workplace, in volunteer situations, and sometimes at home in conversation. Which have you heard? Which do you use?

No, I don't have the authority. (Indirect)
No, I don't have time for that project. (Direct)
No, I don't have time to do this for you. (Direct)
No, we are not able to handle that line of business in our department. (Indirect and Greedy because someone has put rules and attitudes in place to create control and yet has caused an unhelpful attitude toward providing customer service.)

Also, depending on the potential of actually obtaining the resources listed below, the following statements could be a *no*, or a *maybe*. If you really can't get the items, you are saying *no*. If, however, there is a likelihood that you will be able to get what is requested, you are really saying *maybe*.

We don't have the time to do it. (Detailed)
We don't have the staff to do it. (Detailed)
We don't have the budget to do it. (Detailed)
We don't have the facility to do it. (Detailed)
We don't have the equipment to do it. (Detailed)
We don't have people trained to do it. (Detailed)
No money. (Direct)
No budget. (Direct)
No cash flow. (Direct/Detailed)
No authority. (Direct)
No staff time is available. (Direct/Detailed)

The following "all business," very formal ways of saying *no* are heard in some workplaces, in board or shareholder meetings, and in some nonprofit meetings that rely on *Robert's Rules of Order* or another parliamentary authority for governing the meeting.

That plan was voted down. (Direct)
The vote failed. (Direct)
We didn't reach agreement. (Indirect because we still don't know what decision was reached.)

We didn't have a quorum. (Indirect because we don't know what
    happened next.)
The request has been denied. (Direct)
The order was canceled. (Direct)
The request was turned down. (Direct)

The following list is useful for saying *no* to projects, or *no* on behalf
of other people to protect their time.

No, she's not available for that project. (Direct)
No, he doesn't have the skills you need. (Direct)
No, that team isn't free. (Direct)
No, I can't free up that team (or person). They are already assigned.
    (Direct and Detailed)
Nothing further. (Direct)
End of discussion. (Direct)
Over-ruled. (Direct)
That option was thrown out of consideration. (Direct)
That option was eliminated. (Direct)
Abandon the plan. (Direct)
No, I don't know the answer. (Direct)

Rachel, a working woman from Minnesota, shares one of her favorite
ways to say *no*: "No, I am unable to help at this time given my other time
commitments and I would not do your project justice." This example
shows the *detailed* say-no personality in action. And a professional in the
Pacific Northwest shares the realization that "very rarely do I say *no* without offering an option. For example, 'No, I can't meet with you at that
time (I already have lunch plans), but how does the next day work for
you?' or 'No, I would prefer not running the trail at 6 A.M. (it is hard for
me to see in the dark); how about if we do the golf course loop instead?'"
Her say-no personality is a combination of *direct* because she's saying *no*,
and *inspired* because she is confident with her response, knows what she
wants to do, and offers an option that works for her.

## POWER PRACTICE: IDENTIFY THAT SAY-NO PERSONALITY. PART 1

Now it's your turn. Read each statement that follows. Determine which
say-no personality (or combination of say-no personalities) is in action.

Write down the say-no personalities that you see and hear in each statement.

1. "I'd really like to. But I can't."

2. "No. I'm not going to the game tonight."

3. "No. This is a hard decision for me to make. I've thought a lot about it and realize there are not enough hours in the day for me to take this on."

4. "No, I won't be attending. Thank you for the invitation."

5. "No, you can't do that by yourself. I'll have to help you get it done the right way."

6. "No, I'm not up for that today. How about doing that this weekend?"

7. "No, you can't have that all to yourself. I want some."

8. "I don't really want to."

9. "No, we don't have the resources to do this."

10. "No, we won't be attending the party. Jacob and Jenna have soccer games that we committed to attending."

11. "No, I appreciate that you asked me to serve, but this is not the year for me to take anything else on."

12. "No, I'm not in a good spot to talk right now. Can I give you a call back in fifteen minutes?"

13. "No."

14. "No, that purchase can't be made because the money isn't available."

*Answers*

Each statement is identified with its say-no personality. When a better answer could have been given, it is given at the end.

1. "I'd really like to. But I can't." Indirect. More Direct could be: "No. I'd like to, but I can't today."

2. "No. I'm not going to the game tonight." Direct.

3. "No. This is a hard decision for me to make. I've thought a lot about it and realize there are not enough hours in the day for me to take this on." Detailed.

4. "No, I won't be attending. Thank you for the invitation." Gracious.

5. "No, you can't do that by yourself. I'll have to help you get it done the right way." Greedy. A more Direct and Gracious way to negotiate a situation where you want to say something Greedy is to say: "No, I wouldn't suggest doing that way. How about trying it this way . . ."

6. "No, I'm not up for that today. How about doing that this weekend?" Inspired.

7. "No, you can't have that all to yourself. I want some." Greedy. A Direct and Gracious way of restating this sentence: "Will you please share some of that with me?"

8. "I don't really want to." Indirect. "No, I don't want to."

9. "No, we don't have the resources to do this." Direct.

10. "No, we won't be attending the party. Jacob and Jenna have soccer games that we committed to attending." Detailed.

11. "No, I appreciate that you asked me to serve, but this is not the year for me to take anything else on." Gracious.

12. "No, I'm not in a good spot to talk right now. Can I give you a call back in fifteen minutes?" Inspired.

13. "No." Direct.

14. "No, that purchase can't be made because the money isn't available." Detailed.

## POWER PRACTICE: IDENTIFY THAT SAY-NO PERSONALITY. PART 2

Looking for more say-no personality practice? Here are eighteen more opportunities to identify which of the say-no personality types would have said each of the following things.

*Directions*

For each of the following statements, select the single or combined say-no personality that is represented. Choose one or more of these six say-no personalities: Direct, Indirect, Gracious, Detailed, Inspired, or Greedy. Answers follow so that you can test your growing Master of No knowledge.

1. No.

2. You are very kind to think of me, however, no, I am not able to join you.

3. No, you can't take this project over until you've completely trained the new person how to do your job.

4. No, we won't be coming after all. Janey has the chicken-pox and we don't want your kids to get them too.

5. Yes.

6. No one is getting a raise this year. However, no one is getting the same performance review either. Your review is excellent because your work has been above my expectations, on time, and on or under budget. As you know, lay-offs have been occurring based on performance reviews.

7. I don't think I'm the best person for the job.

8. No, I'm not available this week, will next Tuesday at 3 p.m. work?

9. No. Get out of the way. You're slowing the rest of us down.

10. Thank you for the raise. No, it doesn't justify my working more overtime without pay.

11. You'll be happier doing something else.

12. No, I didn't realize we needed $100,000 to fund this project, and we don't have that.

13. You didn't take all of it, did you?

14. I appreciate your offer, I'll take a rain-check.

15. I don't think we're supposed to be talking about this.

16. No. The rules governing our decisions on applications don't allow this exception.

17. No, I didn't see the film. I hear that it's good.

18. No, I never waffle.

*Answers*

1. No. Direct.

2. You are very kind to think of me, however, no, I am not able to join you. Gracious.

3. No, you can't take this project over until you've completely trained the new person how to do your job. Greedy.

4. No, we won't be coming after all. Janey has the chicken-pox and we don't want your kids to get them too. Detailed.

5. Yes. Direct.

6. No one is getting a raise this year. However, no one is getting the same performance review either. Your review is excellent because your work has been above my expectations, on time, and on or under budget. As you know, lay-offs have been occurring based on performance reviews. Inspired.

7. I don't think I'm the best person for the job. Indirect.

8. No, I'm not available this week. Will next Tuesday at 3 p.m. work? Inspired.

9. No. Get out of the way. You're slowing the rest of us down. Greedy.

10. Thank you for the raise. No, it doesn't justify my working more overtime without pay. Gracious.

11. You'll be happier doing something else. Indirect.

12. No, I didn't realize we needed $100,000 to fund this project, and we don't have that. Detailed.

13. You didn't take all of it did you? Greedy.

14. I appreciate your offer. I'll take a rain-check. Gracious.

15. I don't think we're supposed to be talking about this. Indirect.

16. No. The rules governing our decisions on applications don't allow this exception. Detailed.

17. No, I didn't see the film. I hear that it's good. Inspired.

18. No, I never waffle. Direct.

## SAY *NO* GRACIOUSLY

Think of saying *no* not so much as confrontation but as conversation. Conversing or talking with someone is about listening, understanding another person's point of view, and drawing on your knowledge, expertise, skill, and experience in order to share information, insight, or direction. If you believe in something, take a stand; don't avoid a confrontational conversation. Be willing to disagree with others, one-on-one and in group settings. Constructive conflict can be valuable. Sometimes working through why your answer is *no* can bring new solutions or approaches forward in such a way that the *no* stays *no* but a new option is now available that can result in a *yes*.

From the self-assessment in Chapter 1, the phrase "no, thank you" is a gracious way of saying *no*. Other gracious ways to say *no* are:

"I understand your need, my plate is full currently. Here's my
   suggestion on who can assist you . . ." (Gracious, Inspired)
"I'm (we're) not the appropriate person to do this. _____
   is the right person to contact and his/her number
   is _____." (Gracious, Direct)
"No. Thanks for thinking of me." (Gracious)
"No, please take me off your list." (Gracious, Direct)
"No. I'll assign it to _____."(Gracious, Direct)
"No. I'll delegate it to _____." (Gracious, Direct)
"Sorry, no, I can't go with you, I'm doing _____ today."
   (Gracious, Detailed)

Maintain the other person's dignity when you say *no* to a request, an invitation, or a demand. Separate the *no* from the person. Keep the act of saying *no* focused on the request and not on the person who is asking the question. Avoid using the word "you" when saying *no* to a request. You are saying *no* to the request, not the person. Take time to think through what you will say and how you will say it most graciously and least offensively.

According to Marguerite, whom we met earlier in the chapter:

Saying a gracious *no* is an acquired skill, kind of like table manners.
It's a balance between being abrupt or wordy, uncaring or compassionate. It doesn't follow the old rule of "never complain, never explain." I do try to soften a *no* with an explanation, and an alternative if possible. I also own the *no* rather than saying "my boss would not approve it."

Marguerite is describing the language and approaches of a combination of direct, gracious, and inspired say-no personalities.

## Say No *Without Alienating Others*

Even when you are clear, kind, direct, and honest, others can feel alienated from you because you've given them an answer they didn't want to hear: a *no*. Here are some ideas for saying *no* and causing as little disruption or alienation as possible.

1. Be honest and direct. Offer supporting information only when it is factual. You have the power and a right to say *no*. Giving more information than is necessary turns your response into an excuse, which can move you into the waffler-zone and leave you open to saying *yes* at some point in the future.

2. Be gracious. "No, thank you" is both a direct and a gracious phrase.

3. Remember the three levels of saying *no*: 1. No, never; 2. No, maybe; and 3. No, not now, *yes* definitely later. Determine which *no* you want and need to use. Select words that clearly state your meaning without being mean or inconsiderate.

4. When you give a *no* that the requester wasn't prepared to hear, he or she may try to negotiate you away from your *no* answer. Know why you are saying *no*. Own it. Be confident. Don't waffle. Focus your *no* on the issue, not on the person.

5. Should you decide to change your *no* to a *yes*, state clearly what the terms of your saying *yes* are.

## PROTECT TIME AND SPACE FOR DECISION MAKING

Making the decision to say *no* can be a time-consuming and stressful process. Create a space or spaces that are healthy and protected so that you can make good decisions. Select or create a space that is mentally, emotionally, and physically safe, as well as inspiring to the decision-making process. Masters of No seem to live in this space. The rest of us need an actual room, activity, or person to go to.

Just because you have a protected safe space for decision-making doesn't mean you'll use it. So, you also need to protect time for decision making. How much time do you need to make a decision? The time needed to make decisions usually depends on the decision you're faced with making. When in danger, the decision can take from one second to up to a minute. When not in danger, a decision might take a minute or two, all the way up to a day or two. When faced with a life-changing, but not life-threatening, situation, it might take a day, a month, or a year to make a decision.

When the decision and its consequences are complex, more time is required than when the decision and the consequences are not complex. When concerned about how others will react to your decision causes you to delay a decision, you are taking more time than is ethical and fair to the people and situations involved. When presented with something safe, exciting, and interesting to you, you might make the decision in less than a minute. On average, how much time do you spend on making a decision? Is it the right amount of time, too much, or perhaps too little?

## POWER PRACTICE: WHAT WORDS DO YOU USE TO SAY *NO*?

What words do you use to say *no* to the following people? Write down the words you know that you use and the words that you'd like to use to more effectively say *no*.

Your Friends:

Coworkers:

Boss(es):

Your Kids (1 to 3 years of age):

Your Kids (4 to 12 years of age):

Your Kids (13 to 19 years of age):

Your Stepchildren:

Your Spouse:

Your Significant Other:

Your Former Spouse:

Your Date:

Volunteers:

Your Parents:

Your Siblings or Relatives:

## POWER PRACTICE: YOUR BEST SAY-NO SENTENCES

1. What is your best ever say-no sentence?

2. Do you still use it? Why?

3. Do other people understand what you mean when you say this? If not, how can you improve it?

## POLICY OF NO: COMPLETE YOURS

Here's one of the "no, not now, not ever" responses I received when I was reminding people about the opportunity to contribute *no*-stories for this book. The interesting thing is that the responder didn't realize that he'd shared something relevant when he said, "I truly don't have time to make such a contribution now. Meeting a deadline with any quality is not a commitment I can make now." This is a *no* along with language that communicates "I wish I could be giving you a different answer; however, when I'm honest with myself, this is my best answer." This *no* represents a detailed say-no personality.

Once you've recognized your own say-no personality, it's time to revisit your Policy of No statements. The things you don't want to have happen are described in your Policy of No statements. What else don't you want? What else do you want to say *no* to? These are the things you can identify as important and as a part of your values. Your values are a part of your Policy of No.

Consider again what your policies for saying *no* are. You began recording these policies and principles in the last chapter. For instance, "No, you may not stay overnight at Susanna's house when her parents are not home. You know the rules." Or, "I give 10 percent of my time each month to charities, and my time is already committed." Having a set of personal policies that guide your choices can help to remove the personal edge that can be attached to saying *no* to a request. It can also give you confidence to say *no* in words and in body language that those listening to you will take seriously. Having your Policy of No clearly defined allows you to use more effectively the say-no personalities of Direct, Gracious, Detailed, and Inspired. Having your Policy of No in mind allows you to avoid being Indirect and Greedy when you say *no*.

## POWER PRACTICE: **YOUR POLICY OF NO**

1. What are the things you know, without having to think about it, that you will say *no* to?

2. What are your refined and restated Policy of No Statements now?

3. When have your Policy of No Statements worked? What happened?

4. When have your Power of No Statements not worked? What happened?

## SOMETIMES SAYING *NO* DOESN'T WORK

Even when you've applied the Power of No Model, followed your Policy of No, and carefully crafted your No statement, the person hearing your *no* may choose not to accept or respond to it. This happens when the response is not what the person wanted to hear. David Gill, from whom we heard on the subject of ethics in Chapter 4, suggests that saying *no* doesn't work when:

1. When nobody is listening.

2. When people have learned not to trust you.

3. When you feel powerless and are in the presence of arrogant power.

The other situations in which saying *no* doesn't work are the ones in which you've said *no* and then changed your response into a *yes*. When this happens on a regular basis, people stop listening to your *no*'s, and you become a Waffler.

Thankfully the successful stories of saying *no* exist. You have the Power of No Model to help you determine whether to say *no*. Now, what about the words that can be used to say *no*? There are more words and phrases for saying *no* in Appendix C. And of course there are a million or more ways to say *no* because each of us will add different expressions, gestures, and words to show that we mean *no*.

You know you have said *no* in a way that other people understand you mean *no* when:

1. The person doesn't do what you've said *no* to.

2. You stop feeling threatened and start to feel safe again.

3. Your children stop arguing with you.

4. The requester stops bothering you with the same question.

5. The requester thanks you for making a decision.

6. People stop asking you questions.


## POWER PRACTICE: **SAY *NO***

Write down ten ways you can say *no* the next time you want to:

1.

2.

3.

4.

5.

6.

7.

8.

9.

10.

Now, go back and identify the say-no personality you used in each of these ten statements. Then, continue on and imagine what the consequences will be for each of these ways of saying *no*. What are the potential positive, negative, and neutral consequences?

| Say-No Personality Used: | Consequences: |
| --- | --- |
| 1. | |
| 2. | |
| 3. | |
| 4. | |
| 5. | |
| 6. | |
| 7. | |
| 8. | |
| 9. | |
| 10. | |

## THE BOTTOM LINE

According to David Gill, today more than 70 percent of children learn *no* as their first word. "Mama" or "dada" used to be the first words of a child. Now the first words seem to be *no*, followed by "don't," then "mama" or "dada," and, in fifth place, "can't." So what's happened to our adult ability to say *no* easily, at will, with conviction, and determination? We've given up our ability to say *no*. This chapter provided a variety of ways to reclaim your ability to say *no* and to confidently say *no* out loud when *no* is your best response.

## POWER SUMMARY

1. Gather up your confidence and your trust in yourself.

2. Apply the Power of No Model: Purpose, Options, When, Emotional Ties, Rights and Responsibilities.

3. Choose the words you'll use to say *no*. Be aware of your say-no personality and how others may perceive you.

4. Speak the words you choose to use to say *no* out loud, so that others can hear you.

**CHAPTER 6**

# *Stop Saying* Maybe

Make a Decision

## PREVIEW POINTS

1. Recognize the types of waffling.

2. Apply the Power of No Model for improved decision making.

3. Stop waffling: Turn *maybe* into *no*.

## THE WAFFLERS

*Maybe's* are dangerous because the people listening to you rush to conclusions and judgments that may not match our desires to make a decision. *Maybe's* can also be misleading and even unethical if you already know the answer is *yes* or *no*. Wafflers live in the *no-maybe* zone. Using *no-maybe* phrases leaves you on the line and even obligated to still end up doing something at some point.

According to *Merriam-Webster's Collegiate Dictionary*, to waffle is "to vacillate, equivocate, yo-yo, flip-flop, or to talk or write foolishly." And someone who waffles is a waffler. We've all seen wafflers in action and perhaps even waffled ourselves. You know, the person who just can't make a decision or who consistently says "*maybe*" and "we'll see." The person who mentally wavers and doesn't move forward is a waffler. Other waffling behaviors include hesitation in making a choice or committing to a direction, or avoiding a commitment to what is being said.

## Waffling in the News

The words waffle and waffling are used to describe behavior all over the world. Just look at the headlines. In 1993 and again in 1997, "waffling" referred to President Bill Clinton's foreign policy positions. In 2000, "Waffling *no* help" opened a story about dams and waterways in the Western United States. Also in 2000, in *The Times of India* ran a story about relationships between Pakistan and India, titled "No More Waffling." In 2003, Prime Minister Jean Chretien of Canada was reported as "waffling on Iraq" by CBS News.

From 1998 to 2003, the word waffling popped up in stories discussing audits and bookkeeping at major corporations. Waffling in the world of corporate finance means dishonesty, inflating and deflating the numbers and dollars of companies in order to make the financial results look better than they really were.

News stories about the government have described politicians, world leaders, and governmental agencies as "waffling" on policies and decisions. "Telecom waffling at the FCC helm" reported the *Washington Times*, November 26, 2002.

Okay. The case is made. Many of us appear to waffle, or at least get accused of it. But, as your mother might have told you, "Just because everyone jumps off the bridge doesn't mean you should jump too." So, stop waffling and make a decision. Be firm, be clear, and say *no* when you mean *no,* and *yes* when you mean *yes.*

## Why Do We Waffle?

But it's not that easy, is it? So why do we waffle? There are lots of reasons. It can get you out of a hot-seat or sticky situation. You don't have to feel mean or hurt someone. Waffling can also buy you time to gather more information in order to make the best possible decision.

When there is an advantage to waffling, be clear, don't make apologies, and do follow-up with a definite *yes* or *no* when you promised you'd have an answer. Do the research. Ask questions. Apply the Power of No Model. Once you've waffled for a good reason, redeem yourself, keep your promise, and make a decision. But when there is *no* good reason to waffle, don't do it.

## TYPES OF WAFFLING

As we've seen, Wafflers have their own reasons for waffling. There are three types of waffling and you've probably seen them all in action. Or, perhaps you'll recognize yourself in the descriptions that follow.

1. *Flakey Waffler*: You never make a decision.

2. *Waffler*: You are so indirect when you say *no* that people hear you saying *maybe*. Or, you gather information and could make the final decision but for some reason defer the final decision to someone else. For example, even though you have the power to make the decision, you say: "I'll have to check with my manager" or "I have to ask my mom."

3. *Legitimate Waffler*: You are stalling for time so that information can be collected and you can make a good decision. Legitimate-waffling results in a decision in an appropriate amount of time. If the decision takes too long, flakey-waffling has taken over.

When you want decisiveness and leadership from others, you are called upon to demonstrate being decisive in your own life. Waffling has been indirectly described as "the inability to act decisively in the moments that count." Waffling can also be described as postponing a decision indefinitely. Whining about someone else doing something when you've opted not to do anything constructive can also be viewed as waffling. Wafflers are sometimes described as people who don't do much of anything, or who are not doing their fair share of work.

## POWER PRACTICE: IDENTIFY THAT WAFFLER

You've just learned that the three types of wafflers feel differently about their behavior and yet that all three are still waffling.

1. Flakey Waffler: Never decides.

2. Waffler: Needs someone else to make a decision.

3. Legitimate Waffler: Needs time or information to make a decision and who will make a decision when promised.

*Directions*

For each statement below, identify which of the three waffler types—Flakey, Waffler, or Legitimate—is most likely speaking.

1. I don't have the authority to sign.

2. You're kidding right? We can't decide that today.

3. I don't know.

4. I don't know. I'll research it and get you an answer by Tuesday morning.

5. I'll take this to the review committee.

6. Let me think about it.

7. We need the specifications and the deadlines before we make a decision. The bid is due in ten days.

8. I'm not sure.

9. I'm not sure. Let me find out and call (e-mail or fax) you in ten minutes.

10. I want to check in at home before deciding what to do.

*Answers*

1. I don't have the authority to sign. Waffler.

2. You're kidding right? We can't decide that today. Flakey.

3. I don't know. Flakey.

4. I don't know. I'll research it and get you an answer by Tuesday morning. Legitimate.

5. I'll take this to the review committee. Waffler.

6. Let me think about it. Flakey.

7. We need the specifications and the deadlines before we make a decision. The bid is due in ten days. Legitimate.

8. I'm not sure. Flakey.

9. I'm not sure. Let me find out and call (e-mail or fax) you in ten minutes. Legitimate.

10. I want to check in at home before deciding what to do. Waffler.

## POWER PRACTICE: YOUR PERSONAL WAFFLE REVIEW. PART 1

1. When was the last time you waffled?

2. Why did you waffle?

3. What were the consequences of waffling?

4. Whom do you know who is a waffler? Are they Flakey Wafflers, Wafflers, or Legitimate Wafflers?

## CONSEQUENCES OF WAFFLING

*No, maybe* is waffling. When you lack confidence as you say *no*, people listening to you hear a *maybe*. If you use excuses and reasons for your *no* to convince another person that you mean *no*, what tends to be heard is waffling and a belief that "she doesn't really know what she's saying." The indirect say-no personality represents this form of waffling.

Every decision or non-decision has potential consequences. Waffling is a decision you make to *not* make a decision on the question you've been asked. Here are the potential consequences of waffling:

- *Flakey-Waffler Consequences*
  Positive: None.
  Negative: A needed decision doesn't get made. You let others down. You are seen as unable to make decisions. People stop coming to you. People start going where they think decisions will get made. Opportunities are missed. Someone gets hurt.
  Neutral: Whatever you were waffling on didn't end up mattering or causing any problems.

  Flakey-waffling is the most common and most recognized form of waffling. You waffle when you don't want to say *yes* but feel compelled to say *yes*. You waffle when want to say *no* and don't feel comfortable saying *no*. And, you waffle with *maybe*'s when you really don't know whether to say *yes* or *no*.

- *Waffler Consequences*
  Positive: You gather information for someone else to make a decision. You are relied on by the decision maker. He or she makes a decision.
  Negative: People see you as unable to make decisions. The decision maker is a Flakey-Waffler, so no decision gets made. People stop coming to you. People start going where they think decisions will get made. Opportunities are missed. Someone may get hurt. You place blame on someone else as the decision maker. Because people know this about you, they don't respect your decision making, even when you do make a decision.
  Neutral: Whatever you were waffling on didn't end up mattering or causing any problems.

- *Legitimate-Waffler Consequences*
  Positive: You gather the information needed and make a clear *yes* or *no* decision. Once your reputation builds for your follow-through after waffling, people begin to respect you more.

Negative: If you don't follow through by the promised response-deadline, you are back to square one, being a Flakey Waffler.

Neutral: A decision was made. No one is upset with you. No one got hurt. No harm occurred during the delay.

## POWER PRACTICE: WHEN WAFFLING WORKED FOR YOU

1. When have you waffled, then followed through and made a decision?

2. What happened? How did things work out?

3. Who was affected by your waffling? Was anyone not able to get their part of a project done while they waited on you?

4. When have your kids waffled and gotten you to make a decision for them? What usually happens? What do you usually do?

## WORDS FROM THE POWER OF NO SELF-ASSESSMENT: INTERPRETATION

"*No—maybe later.*" The Wafflers live here, mostly saying *maybe* in the following or similar ways. The seven "*maybe*" statements from the Power of No Self-Assessment are described further below. The numbers match the question number from the Self-Assessment.

| What You Say | What Others Hear |
|---|---|
| 2. Couldn't you find someone else? | I'll do it if you can't find someone else. |
| 5. My schedule doesn't allow me to take that on right now. | I can't do it now but might do it later. |
| 8. I'm sorry I can't help out. | I care about your request, so I might help you out at another time. |
| 11. I don't think I'm the best person for this. | Find someone else, but I can do it if you don't find someone else. |
| 14. *Maybe* later. | I'll do it later. |

| 17. *Maybe.* | It could be *yes* and it could be no, or it could be that I'll never make a decision. |
| --- | --- |
| 20. I think I've already taken on too much. | I feel overwhelmed but I'm not saying *no*. |

## No—Maybe: *What Other People Hear*

In the review of the seven self-assessment statements above, we discovered a variety of *maybe* phrases. These *maybe* or Waffler phrases leave you on the line to still end up having to do something. Let's look at some other meanings of *maybe* statements.

> "Maybe." You think you are saying no or at least buying time. I don't hear no but hear "yes, at some point I will do that for you."
> "Maybe?" Spoken as a question, the word maybe becomes agreement and then a yes.
> "Maybe!" You are undecided so you excitedly say *maybe*. This too I hear as a *yes*.
> "No?" You are hesitant with your no, so I hear *maybe*.
> "Please place your request right here" (tactfully said while pointing at your in-box). You haven't said *yes* or no to my request yet.
> "We do not have the required information to provide a quote." You are telling me *yes* because if I bring the required information, you will provide a quote.

## Turn Maybe *into* No

If you use the above sentences on a regular basis, it's time to stop: time to stop waffling and start being decisive by turning these *maybe's* into *no's*. Here's how. In the list the follows, circle the *maybe* phrases you use and remember that to turn them into *no* statements, all you have to do is say *no*.

> "Maybe."—No.
> "Maybe?"—No.
> "Maybe!"—No.
> "No?"—No.
> "No, not now, *maybe* later."—No.
> "Not now, *maybe* later."—No.
> "No, let's reschedule."—No, I am not able to meet with you.

"Is it important enough that I should drop everything else?"—No, I have other priorities.

"I would like to but my other priorities are to get task A and project B done."—No, I have other priorities.

"I can't fit it in."—No, I can't fit it in.

"I can't fit it into my schedule right now. Check back with me."—No, I can't fit it in.

"I can't complete this within your time frame."—No, I can't complete it in your time frame.

"I'm sorry, I just can't at this time."—No, I can't.

"I don't have time."—No, I don't have time.

"I don't have time right now."—No, I don't have time.

## POWER PRACTICE: TURN YOUR *MAYBE'S* INTO *No's*

1. What are your favorite "maybe" statements?

2. Rewrite them as "no" statements.

3. Now, rewrite your favorite Waffler statements as "yes" statements.

## POWER PRACTICE: TURN YOUR WAFFLING STATEMENTS INTO *NO*

The following statements are waffling statements because when you use them, you are not telling me *no*, you are trying to get me to ask someone else for help. So, each of these statements can be replaced with something similar to "No, I'm not the best person for this and so I will not help out."

Is there someone else available to do it?
Someone else with better expertise in this area could do it.
Someone else with better expertise in this area should do it.
I'm not the right person. Maybe _____ could do it.
I don't have the right skills. Maybe _____ could do it.
I'm not the right person for that, _____ really likes to do that.
Is there anyone else who can get this for you?

## THE POWER TO END WAFFLING AND BECOME DECISIVE

The good news is that you can overcome waffling. You can learn how to make better decisions by relying on a series of questions that will lead you to a clear *yes*, a clear *no*, or a clear commitment to what needs to happen before you can arrive at a clear answer.

In Chapter 2, the Power of No Model was presented as a tool for making decisions based on gaining a clear understanding of the five POWER areas. When you keep a requester talking with you about the five POWER areas, you can gather enough information to reach a clear *yes* or *no* decision. Remember to gather as many details as you can about the Purpose-, Options-, and When-timeframes of the request, your Emotional Ties to the request, and your Rights and Responsibilities.

Information gathering is important to your decision-making process. However, at some point, the time is up and you need to make a decision. Or, you reach a point where you've gathered enough information to make a decision and move on.

Use the Power of No Model to stop waffling and be decisive. Here's how: Ask yourself and others enough questions at each of the five POWER decision points to determine what your best answer or response is. Otherwise, you'll get stuck waffling again.

### Purpose

Remember that the *Purpose* of a request is the clear statement of what is wanted or needed, why it is wanted, and how it relates to the goals to be accomplished. When you feel like waffling because the Purpose isn't clear, ask questions such as these:

- What is it that needs to be done?
- Why am I the best person to help with this?
- What will we be able to accomplish as a result of doing this?

### Options and Resources

Once you understand the purpose of the request, it is time to find out what options and resources are available to you. Remember that *Options* are what you choose from to get things done. Options are about how you get things done. And *Resources* are about what and who is available to help get things done. Resources are the tools, people, equipment, finances, and authority-levels available to help complete the request. Ask questions such as these to explore what options and resources really are available to you so that you can stop waffling and make a decision:

- Can someone else take on the assignment?
- How many ways can the task be completed?
- What tools, equipment, and money will be available to help complete the request?
- Who is available to help? Or, How many volunteers or workers can help?

Also remember that if the options and resources available to you don't allow for a successful result, now is the time to say *no*. If options and resources are available to help get things done, it's time to move on to the next decision-point and discover when the project or request is due and whether you'll say *yes* or *no* to the project or request.

## When

A statement of *When* a request needs to be completed tells you the timing of the project, or the deadline of the request for help. To determine when the request needs to be done, ask the following questions:

- What specific date and time does this need to be done?
- Is the deadline fixed, negotiable, or a floating/changing deadline?
- Will this timeframe work with everything else we have to do?
- Will the timing of this request allow for the needed resources to be available?

## Emotional Ties

*Emotional Ties* grow from your past experiences, from your intuitive sense of how the project or request will work out, or from an unexplained sense of not wanting to do something. Remember that emotions may prompt excitement, commitment, and energy for saying *yes* to a request. On the other hand, emotions may prompt resentment, distrust, and energy for saying *no* to a request.

Decision-points one through three—Purpose, Options, and When—are logical. You reason through each of them, negotiating where needed. Yet even with all that logical discussion, your emotions can cause you to waffle and affect whether you'll actually commit to saying *yes* or *no*.

After you look at a request clearly and thoroughly, consider how you feel. Ask:

- What is it that you really want to do, accomplish, or be involved with?
- How will you feel if you say *no*?
- How will you feel if you say *yes*?

Then determine what your best response to a request really is: *yes* or *no*.

### Rights and Responsibilities.

*Rights* are the things that can be claimed as true about a situation and the things that will continue to be true whether you say *yes*, or *no* to a request. Along with your rights, learn what *Responsibilities* you will be accountable for. Responsibilities are the legal, moral or mental accountabilities or duties that you will be expected to live up to, deliver on, and perform to.

Once you've decided to say *yes* or *no*, you want to confirm that you will be protected and supported in your decision. Ask questions such as these so that you know what support you can expect as you follow through on carrying out your *yes* or *no* decision:

- What will happen to me if I say *no*?
- What can I expect to stay the same if I say *yes*?
- What am I responsible for if I say *yes*?
- What am I responsible for if I say *no*?

After you've explored and discussed these questions completely, your best *yes* or *no* response becomes clear. Because of an in-depth discussion before making your decision, you will be more likely to follow through on your decision. And, you'll have greater protection during the process of completing the request because you've confirmed what your rights and responsibilities are as those around you see them.

## OKAY TO WAFFLE?

When is it okay or even healthy to waffle? When you need more information to make a decision and you will make the decision. When you don't have authority to make the decision and need a decision or an approval from someone else before you can move forward. Stop putting decisions off. Your waffling is inconsiderate to those relying on you to make a decision and take action.

Making decisions requires both thought and action. Saying *maybe* leaves you in a state of limbo and leaves you positioned to do nothing. Saying "I can't afford to" is still a decision. Couldn't you find the money if it was really important? Saying "I don't have enough time" is still a decision. Could you find a way to make "enough time?"

My first recollection of "I don't have enough time" comes from elementary school. I remember mom coming home from work and saying, "I don't have enough time, and you girls are going to have to help me." For some reason, I rebelled—internally—against that phrase. I helped, but I remembered the dreaded phrase. Now I understand why. "I don't have enough time" is a waffling phrase used in this case to enlist help. How much time we feel we have is a choice. The choice is to say *yes* to so many things for which you feel that you don't have enough time, or to say *no* to the right number of things so that you feel that you have the right number of hours in the day.

Related to this story is the story of another woman, Lisa, who shared that her husband came home for four or five months saying, "I don't have enough time to get everything done." He was more and more tired, and less and less interested in doing things with her. His reasoning was that the load at work was too much, the boss wasn't helping, and no one else knew how to do things the right way. So, "he had to go in early and stay late." Lisa's frustration was that he was acting like a victim, talking like there were no choices. Lisa tried to say "you do have a choice" and all he'd respond with was, "You just don't understand." Finally, in her tiredness, Lisa said to him, "Next time you say that you don't have enough time, I'm going to ignore you. You have a choice and every time you say that you don't have enough time I find myself feeling more and more stress. We always have a choice about how we handle things."

Months went by. Many activities and conversations occurred. Life was lived. One day, Lisa's husband, who had been a Marine, said during a conversation, "I realize that even during my time in the Marines I had a choice. I didn't think that I had a choice but I did. If I was told to do something, I didn't have to do it. Of course, there were consequences for not doing things, so we all chose to do it, whatever 'it' was. We also were told that if we were commanded to do something that was against the law, we could refuse to do it. I never thought about it like this. I never thought about having a choice. Now I realize that I had a choice then, just as I do now. I can choose to stay working in this environment that makes me tired and frustrated, I can move to another job, or I can focus on improving the situation I'm in."

There is always a choice. Here's a "choice" story that I've shared with conference attendees. In 2002, I invested ten weeks of my life in training at the police academy—living, eating, studying, driving, shooting, researching, and reporting. One of the lessons I learned during my time at the academy is "make the decision to never give up. You always have an option. Even when threatened you have an option. Even when in a remote location you have an option. Even when negotiating with people you have options. And even down on your knees with a gun to the back of your head, you have an option." The point is to make a choice, to make a decision.

Thankfully, you aren't faced with such dangerous daily situations. You are, however, faced daily with decisions. For instance, during a college internship I worked with a team of women who were already married, had children, and had worked for the company for a number of years. One day over lunch, two of the women were complaining about their work environment, the boss, the lack of raises, and the commute time. I on the other hand was enjoying the work, what I was learning, and the range of people I was meeting. I said to them, "If you dislike this job so much, why don't you look for another one?" The lady with near-college-age children said, "You don't understand. Someday you will. When you have a mortgage to pay, kids to clothe and feed, and put through college."

My coworker's implication was that she "had no choice" but to keep her job. The fact is that she was making a choice to keep the job. She had already made hundreds of choices that led to her choosing to keep her job. She'd made choices to buy a house, have a mortgage, have children, send them to college, have a car, go on vacations, and was choosing to believe that she wouldn't find another job with equal benefits. For her, the total of these choices led to choosing to stay where she was, and to complain about it. Her behavior was a form of waffling: complaining and not taking action to improve things.

## POWER PRACTICE: YOUR PERSONAL WAFFLE REVIEW. PART 2

1. What choices have you made that cause you to waffle and be indecisive?

2. What mindsets prevent you from making decisions?

3. Which of your emotions cause you to waffle and say *maybe*?

## THE TEENAGE EXCEPTION

Years ago, my friend Judy's teenage daughter was on the phone talking to one of her friends while Judy and I were talking in the kitchen. I heard

Judy's daughter use a "warmed-waffle" and say, "I have to ask my mom." Of course, Judy and I then had a conversation about the use of "I have to ask my mom." To me it seems that asking for permission was good when needed, that relying on "mom" to make a decision that the daughter could have made on her own seemed like a weakness—or a waffling position. Judy explained that she was "happy to be the decision maker so that my daughter doesn't get rejected by a friend." So there is a time for waffling with "I have to ask someone else."

Except for a few special cases, ultimately waffling is dangerous because:

1. You end up saying *yes* when you meant to say *no*.

2. You never follow through to make a clear decision.

3. You miss out on opportunities.

4. Someone gets hurt because of your indecision.

When you rely on waffling as your only decision tool, you give up your ability to make a decision. Said another way, unused skills atrophy and disappear. So, stop waffling.

## POWER PRACTICE: STOP WAFFLING, SAY *NO*

The statements that follow are also waffling because you are not telling me *no*, you are on the tasks to be done, or negotiating for time. Really you are telling me that if the details can be changed, you'll say *yes*. Beware of these *maybe's*! Turn them into *no's* (for example, "No, I don't have time to help you.").

For the following statements, write down what you'll say instead:
I'm bogged down right now, can this wait?

Can it wait?

Can't it wait?

Do you have to have that now?

This is my priority list. You let me know what the priorities are for me to work on.

Here's my project load. What would you have me drop to take on this project?

Which project is most important to you?

I'm working on other high priority projects at this time and do not have time.

"Failure to plan on your part does not constitute crisis on my part." (original source unknown)

You wanted it when?

Would it be okay if I recommended someone else?

Would it be okay if I delegated this?

I can do this if I don't do _____. Which one is more important?

Send me an e-mail with what is needed and when.

If you want me to do this, I will need _____ and _____ first.

This will put me into overtime.

You didn't have an appointment.

I'm not making a decision today.

I don't have the budget now.

### Potential Answers

Compare your answers to the potential answers listed here. Yours may be just as strong, as long as the word *no* is in your response. The responses that follow are primarily direct say-no approaches, so they may feel too direct for your say-no personality.

I'm bogged down right now, can this wait? "No. I'm not free to do this right now."

Can it wait? "No. I'm not going to stop what I'm working on."

Can't it wait? "No. I'm not going to delay my current project."

Do you have to have that now? "No, I'm not at a stopping point. Could we schedule another time to look at it?"

This is my priority list. You let me know what the priorities are for me to work on. "No, I'm not clear on what the priorities are anymore. So, let's look at my list and decide what would need to drop off so that I can help you."

Here's my project load. What would you have me drop to take on this project? "No, I'm not convinced that my project load can be lightened. Here's the list, what would you have me drop?"

Which project is most important to you? "No, I'm not clear. Which project is most important to you?"

I'm working on other high priority projects at this time and do not have time. "No, I don't have time."

Failure to plan on your part does not constitute crisis on my part. "No, I'm not going to drop everything to help you."

You wanted it when? "No, I can't meet your deadline."

Would it be okay if I recommended someone else? "No, I'm not going to take this on. I'll recommend someone else."

Would it be okay if I delegated this? "No, I'm not going to take this on. I'll recommend someone else."

I can do this if I don't do _____. Which one is more important? "No, I'm not clear. Which project is most important to you?"

Send me an e-mail with what is needed and when. "No, I'm not understanding what you want. If you'll send me an e-mail with what you need and when you need it, then I'll respond within four hours."

If you want me to do this, I will need _____ and _____ first. "No. I won't do this because everything we need to get this done is not available."

This will put me into overtime. "No, I'm not going to do this on overtime."

You didn't have an appointment. "No, I'm not going to see you without an appointment."

I'm not making a decision today. "No, I'm not making a decision today. I'll let you know by 3 p.m. tomorrow."

I don't have the budget now. "No. There is no budget."

## COMMONLY SEEN WAFFLER SIGNS

Think about the waffler signs we see nearly every day. These are signs that are warning us, inviting us to use caution, and to make our own decisions about how to proceed.

"Beware of Dog" means you can enter at your own risk because the dog might bother or even harm you. This is certainly not a welcome mat, nor is it a go-away sign. It is a waffler-warning sign, unlike "No trespassing" or "No Soliciting"—both of which mean go-away and are clear *no*-statements.

"Enter at Your Own Risk" means that you may enter, but that whoever posted the sign is not responsible for you or your safety. The suggestion is that you may not be safe if you choose to enter. This sign is a warning that leaves room for you to make a decision to enter or not enter.

"Caution. Hot." This sign follows suit. You are being warned and yet also being given permission to make your own decision about what you'll do with the "hot" information.

"Drive with Care" means that the driving conditions ahead are potentially dangerous. No one wants you to get hurt, so a warning is posted. You get to decide whether you'll keep driving or turn around. You also get to decide how you'll drive.

Choices. Every day you are faced with choices. Every time you choose to waffle, you are giving up other choices. What are you going to choose from now on?

## POWER PRACTICE: TURN *MAYBE'S* INTO A NO OR A YES.

Turn these *maybe* phrases into *no-never* sentences. Write down what you'll say the next time you need to say *no* and are tempted to say *maybe*.

| Mostly Maybe | No, Never |
|---|---|
| Maybe. | |
| Maybe? | |
| Maybe! | |
| No? | |
| No, not now, maybe later. | |
| Not now, maybe later. | |

| | |
|---|---|
| No, let's reschedule. | |
| Is it important enough that I should drop everything else? | |
| I'm sorry, I just can't at this time. | |
| My schedule is booked. | |

Now turn these same phrases into *yes* phrases.

| Mostly Maybe | Yes |
|---|---|
| Maybe. | |
| Maybe? | |
| Maybe! | |
| No? | |
| No, not now, maybe later. | |
| Not now, maybe later. | |
| No, let's reschedule. | |
| Is it important enough that I should drop everything else? | |
| I'm sorry, I just can't at this time. | |
| My schedule is booked. | |

*Potential Answers*

Turn these *maybe's* into a *no*.

| Mostly Maybe | No, Never |
|---|---|
| Maybe. | No. |
| Maybe? | No. |
| Maybe! | No. |
| No? | No. |
| No, not now, maybe later. | No. |
| Not now, maybe later. | No. |

| No, let's reschedule. | No. |
|---|---|
| Is it important enough that I should drop everything else? | No, I won't do that for you. |
| I'm sorry, I just can't at this time. | No. |
| My schedule is booked. | No. |

Now turn these same phrases into *yes* phrases.

| *Mostly Maybe* | Yes. |
|---|---|
| Maybe. | Yes. |
| Maybe? | Yes. |
| Maybe! | Yes. |
| No? | Yes. |
| No, not now, maybe later. | Yes, I'll do that in two hours. |
| Not now, maybe later. | Yes, I'd like to do that in three months. |
| No, let's reschedule. | Yes, let's reschedule. |
| Is it important enough that I should drop everything else? | Yes, I'll rearrange so that I can help out for two hours. |
| I'm sorry, I just can't at this time. | Yes, I'll find a way to help you. |
| My schedule is booked. | Yes, I'll rearrange my schedule to find one hour to help you. |

## POWER PRACTICE: PEOPLE AND YOUR DECISIONS

1. When you are indecisive, who supports your waffling?
2. When you are indecisive, who stands up to you and asks you to make clear choices?
3. From now on, what will you do to stop waffling?

## THE BOTTOM LINE

Waffling means to talk or boast of something and yet not take action or not change the situation. Waffling is a choice to not make a decision. The former Marine waffled with "I don't have enough time." The coworker waffled with "I can't just change jobs." Do you do waffle too?

Here's an example of waffling from a person who wanted to contribute a story for this book. "NO! I have *no* time to share a story! How's that? Actually, I would be more than happy to respond if you can allow me until May. April is more than hectic." The statement started out as a direct say-no, with an explanation. The "NO! I have *no* time" is both a logical and an emotional response to the invitation to share a story. Then the "actually" sentence turned into a negotiated *yes,* "if you can allow me until May." The "yes" part of the paragraph is an emotional response based on wanting to focus on saying *no* more effectively, helping out, and sharing a story. In one short paragraph, the direct say-no *no* and the indirect say-no *yes* add up to a *maybe.*

Every day you are faced with questions, choices, and decisions, from what to wear to how to make the final project decision at work. And *no* matter how many decisions you made *yes*terday, there are more to make today, and still more to make tomorrow. Stop waffling, be decisive, and move on.

## POWER SUMMARY

1. Gather up your confidence and trust in yourself.

2. Use the Power of No Model decision-making tool and questions to have a discussion that allows you to gather more information and make a decision.

3. Choose the words you'll use to say *yes* or *no.*

4. Say the words out loud.

5. Keep your resolve.

## CHAPTER 7

# *Saying* Yes

## POWER PREVIEW POINTS

1. *No* for now, means *yes*, later.

2. Internal and external matches.

3. Masters of No know when to say *yes*.

## *No* for Now

"*No*, I'm not able to help you now. I am interested in the activity and would like to participate later." This is a valid and honest way of saying *no* for now, however I'll say *yes* later. As discussed in Chapter 5, an indirect *no* is usually heard as a *maybe* or a *yes*. In this chapter, the focus is on saying *yes*—creating an internal/external match so that it becomes easy to follow through on *yes* and so that you don't fall back into being a Waffler. Masters of No know when to say *yes* and when to say *no*. Wafflers have no idea, and *Yes*-ism people are locked into saying *yes* to everything and everyone.

You know you've said *yes* too much when any of these things start to happen to you:

1. You keep yourself awake at night worrying about all that you have to do.

2. You feel tired nearly all of the time.

3. You don't get done all of the things you've promised to do.

4. You often say things like "I don't have enough time!"

5. Other people stop asking you to do things because you don't follow through.

6. Other people have expressed concern about your well-being, because you always seem so busy and tired.

## SAYING *YES*: THE INTERNAL AND THE EXTERNAL

The internal part of saying *yes* involves your thoughts and your actions, and your internal desires. The external part of saying *yes* involves your externalized behavior and spoken responses. When you have an internal and external match, your mind, heart, and instinct say *yes,* and your mouth, eyes, and body language also say *yes.* There are two types of internal/external say-yes scenarios.

The first is a match—you want to say *yes* or *no* in your head and you say that out loud. For example, you want to go to the game and so you say *yes, I'll go.* Or, you want to say *yes* to the new assignment, and so you say *yes, thank you, I would like to accept the assignment.*

The second is a mismatch because you want to say *no* and yet you finding yourself saying *yes* out loud. A mismatch happens, for example, when you don't have time to take anything else on and in your head and heart you really want to say *no,* but because you feel that others will see you as mean if you say *no* or for some other reason, you end up saying *yes* out loud.

For *Yes*-ism people and Wafflers, the ability to match internal and external "answers" is difficult at best. For every two times that you want to say *yes* or *no,* you typically find yourself actually saying out loud what you internally want to say only once. In the paragraphs that follow, you'll discover the *yes* matches and mismatches and why they happen.

## INTERNAL / EXTERNAL MATCH

In your head you want to say *yes,* so you say *yes* out loud. This is an internal/external match because what you are internally feeling and thinking is what you say externally or out loud. Even when you're clear on the match, knowing that you've said *yes* out loud and in your mind, others may not hear your *yes.*

Even though the word *yes* came out of your mouth, did the people you said it to hear *maybe.* Here's what I mean. "Yes?" is a question rather than a statement and can mean that you are really saying *maybe.* "Yes?" can also mean that you are acknowledging someone else. Depending on the tone of voice you use, "Yes!" can be agreement or it can be a demand.

"Yes! I'd love to go with you to the movie" is agreement. "Yes! I will make you clean up your room" is a demand. Once you've said *yes*, follow through and do what you've promised so that others recognize your statement of *yes* as *yes* and your *no* as *no*.

*No* is a complete sentence. *Yes* is also a complete sentence. When you say *yes*, you are committing to take action or you are confirming something. Be ready to back up your *yes* with your actions.

## POWER PRACTICE: SAYING YES

1. How do you say *yes*?

2. What does your face look like?

3. What does your voice sound like?

4. How do you stand or sit?

5. How do others hear you saying *yes*? As a *yes*, a *maybe*, an acknowledgment, or a question?

6. When do you say *yes* as an agreement?

7. When do you say *yes* as a demand?

### Internal / External Mismatch

This is the *Don't-Want-To* Mismatch: You want to say *no* because you don't want to do what's been requested, but you say *yes* out loud.

You say *yes* out loud even though you don't want to for dozens of reasons. When you are afraid, or don't like the consequences of saying *no*, you'll say *yes*. For example, "If I say *no* to my boss, I'll loose my job." You also create a mismatch when you don't like the task but say *yes* and do it because you want to be helpful. A teenager shared this example, "I don't like making the dinner-salad, yet I know it needs to be made so that we can eat dinner. So, I make the salad."

Mismatched *yes* statements can also include:

You don't want to go to the meeting for your boss, but you say *yes*.
You don't want your children to go to a friend's for dinner, but you haven't said *yes* in such a long time that you say *yes* this time because you know the friend's parents are home.
You don't want to go to a movie but you can't think of anything better to do, so you say *yes* and go to the movie.

## An External / Internal Mismatch

This is the *Want-To* Mismatch: You want to say *yes*, yet you say *no* out loud.

You say *no* out loud when you really want to say *yes* for a variety of reasons and in a variety of circumstances. For example, a person who's been asked to go to a movie he really wants to see says, "No, I want to go, but I have already committed to watching the kids for the whole weekend." Or, a team member who has been offered a long awaited and desired promotion says, "No, my life situation is such that I'm not able to commit to a new position."

Can you eliminate the mismatches? No, because there will continue to be times when something you don't like to do, haven't learned to do, or don't want to do is important. And so when you recognize that the request is important to a process, a project, or another person, you will internally think *no, I don't want to,* but externally say *yes.* And there will continue to be times when something you've really wanted or wanted to do is offered to you at a time when it doesn't work out.

## POWER PRACTICE: CREATING MATCHES

1. What was your most frustrating or disappointing *yes* mismatch experience?

2. What happened?

3. How would you handle it differently now?

4. What will you do next time you start to say *yes* without planning to follow-through? (Remember, ethics and credibility go hand-in-hand.)

## CREATING *YES* STATEMENTS THAT MEAN *YES*

Although there isn't a way to completely eliminate the mismatches, there is a way to reduce the number of mismatch experiences. You can use the Power of No Model to make sure your *yes* responses are as clear as your *no* responses. In other words, you can create *yes* statements that mean *yes.* Here's how the Power of No Model applies to saying *yes:*

## Purpose

The *Purpose* of a request is the clear statement of what is wanted or needed, why it is wanted, and how it relates to the goals to be accomplished. When the Purpose or a request is clear, internally you can say *yes* and externally you can continue the discussion to explore the remaining four parts of the Power of No Model.

## Options and Resources

Remember that *Options* are what you choose from to get things done. Options are about how you get things done. And *Resources* are about what and who is available to help get things done. Resources are the tools, people, equipment, finances, and authority-levels available to help complete the request. When you are confident that the right options and resources will be available to you as you complete the request or Purpose, then you can internally say *yes* and externally continue the discussion to find out When it is due.

## When

A statement of *When* a request needs to be completed tells you the timing of the project, or the deadline of the request for help. If the time frames and deadline are realistic and you have the Options and Resources needed, then you can say *yes* internally and explore how you feel before making your final decision.

## Emotional Ties

*Emotional Ties* can grow from your past experiences, from your intuitive sense of how the project or request will work out, or from an unexplained sense of not wanting to do something. After you've explored and discussed the POW parts of the Power of No Model, consider how you really feel about the responses you've been given. Ask yourself whether you really want to say *yes* out loud. Just because you've said *yes* internally to the first three areas of discussion, doesn't mean that you feel like you want to take the project on.

## Rights and Responsibilities.

*Rights* are the things that can be claimed as true about a situation and the things that will continue to be true when you say *yes* to a request. Along with your rights, learn what responsibilities you will be accountable for. *Responsibilities* are the legal, moral or mental accountabilities or duties that you will be expected to live up to, deliver on, and perform to. Once you've said *yes*, you want to continue your conversation and confirm that you will be protected and supported in your *yes* decision.

## SAYING *YES* OUT LOUD

When building a *yes* statement that means *yes*, you want all *YES* answers to the Power of No Model questions that follow.

1. **P**urpose: Does the word *yes* appear in the sentence?

2. **O**ptions and Resources: Do you know what your options and resources are to help get this done?

3. **W**hen: Does the sentence say clearly when your *yes* takes effect?

4. **E**motional Ties: Have you acknowledged how you feel about what you are going to say?

5. **R**ights: Have you considered your rights, responsibilities, and the consequences of saying *yes*?

If you can't say *yes* to all five of these questions, you may be putting yourself in the *maybe*-waffler position, a position in which others may think you are not answering or are saying *no*. If you find yourself saying *no* to any of these questions, ask for more information that will help you discover the details of each of the five Powers of No. Then, revisit these five questions and make your clear internal *yes* or *no* decision so that you can state your best response out loud and follow through.

## SAY WHAT YOU MEAN

Sometimes it happens, even when you've applied the Power of No Model to your decision-making process. You didn't want to say *yes*, but you said *yes*. Now you realize that you need to say *no*, so you say *no* out loud. This changing of what you've said out loud causes frustration on everyone's part and can cause confusion. When this happens, be prepared for people to be unhappy with you if you change your *yes* to a *no*.

For instance, in the "Own it" story in Chapter 4, teacher and consultant Brenda held one of her students accountable with these words:

"Owning" your choices, responses, and actions means that you know why you've made your decision, that you know at least some of the consequences, and that you are committed to the response you gave. About one-third of the people I talk with speak of "owning" their *no* responses and their decisions. As difficult as *no* is to say, when you don't own the *no*, someone else can talk you out of your response. When you are talked out of your response, you end up being seen as a Waffler.

When options and circumstances change, and your *no* changes to a *yes*, you still have an opportunity to own your decisions and your response. Take a look at the following story from Jim, who while running for public office, worked through a change-up process of letting his original *no* response become a *yes*. His story also shows The Power of No Model in action. Can you find each of the five Power elements in his story?

During my working career, I also felt that I should be involved in the community and give service in that way. Thus, I decided to run for public office. The first term that I ran for office was a hotly-contested race; however, I was one of the two winners.

Shortly after starting to serve in that office, I learned that there were problems with the chief administrator. I worked very hard to understand the various parts of the problems; however, the gulf widened and there was a real threat to harmony in the community, as well as to the services provided by the public institution. During the second year of my three-year term, I was elected the chair of the governing body. Shortly thereafter, the chief administrator left and the search was on for a replacement. A very strong administrator was hired.

During this last year of my term, I decided that I was finished with such demanding public service, so I decided that I would not run for a second term. *No,* I said and *No* I meant. When the new chief administrator and my supporters heard that I did not want to run, a delegation of supporters came to me and asked if I would run again.

After much soul-searching, including talking with my family, I finally said they could put my name on the ballot, with one caveat: I would not campaign for the position. The supporters ran the campaign. When the election results were in, I had received two out of every three votes cast for that office. I then served a very fruitful and more harmonious three-year term the second time around. I was grateful to feel rewarded for the community service that I provided to the community.

The morale to my story? Saying *no* in the beginning, might not end up as *no*.

## THE MODELS IN ACTION

Did you spot the Power of No Model in action in this man's story? Here's the play-by-play of the model.

1. **P**urpose: Serve the community. Work for the good of the family, of the board, and of the community.

2. **O**ptions: "If I run, I'm not campaigning" and "the supporters ran the campaign."

3. **W**hen: "During the campaigning process I won't be involved." And the length of service was a known quantity of three years from the time of being sworn into office.

4. **E**motional Ties: Used "soul-searching" to make a decision. Wanted "harmony" on the board and in the community.

5. **R**ights and Responsibilities: This man was clear on what he felt was a responsibility—"serving the community"—and on what his "won't campaign" rights were to protect his own energy.

   This man's story talks about a spoken *no* turning into a spoken *yes*. "The most frustrating *no*'s are those that are never said," says Marguerite Mason. "These unspoken '*no*'s' come from people who can't or won't face the issue head on. So, instead of saying *no* they go ahead and do the thing they wanted to do in the way they wanted to do it." She adds that "getting to *no* implies that someone made a request in the first place. Because hearing *no* was a frequent and unpleasant occurrence for me as a child, I tend to do as many things as possible without asking for help. Aside from being an ingrained habit at this point in my life, it cuts down on the potential for hearing a *no*."

   The point is to say what you mean the first time so that you don't end up changing your mind later. Use the Power of No questions to say what you mean in the first place.

## POWER PRACTICE: MASTERS OF NO ARE MASTERS OF YES TOO

Masters of No know when to say *no* and when to say *yes*. Masters of No know clearly why they say *no* and why they say *yes*. Masters of No don't get caught waffling and Masters of No only say *yes* when they absolutely mean *yes*. Think about the people you work with, your family members, and your friends. Then respond to the questions that follow:

1. Whom do you know who knows when to say *yes* and when to say *no*?

2. Of these people, whom could you ask for help in order to overcome your Yes-ism?

3. Whom do you know who is a Yes-ism person?

4. How will you start helping him or her learn to say *no*?

## THE CONSEQUENCES OF SAYING *YES*

In Chapter 4, there was a discussion of consequences and how they affect our decision making. Saying *yes* can have positive, negative, and neutral consequences. Just as you'll consider the consequences of saying *no* you'll consider the consequences of saying *yes*. Whether you say *yes* or *no*, you want to be able to say your answer confidently and then follow through on what you've said. Considering the consequences of your response will help you to make the best possible decisions and increase your success in following through.

The *positive consequences* of saying *yes* include getting what you want, helping others get what they want, enjoying activities, learning something new, feeling happy, and getting to spend time with people you like.

The *negative consequences* of saying *yes* include taking on too much work, committing to being in too many places with too many people, wearing out, feeling tired all of the time, and not getting everything done that you've committed to so that you end up letting other people down.

The *neutral consequences* of saying *yes* include *no* one gets angry or overly excited with you, you don't feel upset or happy about what you've committed to, and nothing bad happens.

## POWER PRACTICE: CONSEQUENCES OF YES

1. When have you experienced the positive consequences of saying *yes*? What happened?

2. When have you experienced the neutral consequences of saying *yes*?

3. When have you experienced the negative consequences of saying *yes?*

## THE ETHICS OF *YES*

We've all said *yes* without thinking. *Yes* to a cause we favor, *yes* to a child to get them to be quiet, and *yes* because we were distracted. Sometimes *yes* responses work in your favor. Other times your *yes* responses work against you, giving you too much work to do or too many places to be at one time. And on occasion, you might have said *yes* when you had *no* intention of following through on the commitment. In Chapter 4, we talked about the ethics of *no*. There is also an ethics of *yes*. When you say *yes* and don't follow through, you are breaking a promise, letting people down, and potentially losing your credibility. Here are some questions to answer when testing the honesty and ethics of your *yes*.

1. Will you follow through?

2. Will everyone's needs get met fairly well?

3. Will everyone be safe?

4. Will the task be completed on time and as promised?

5. Do you feel good about saying *yes?*

When you have all YES answers to these questions, yes is likely an honest answer. If you have any NO answers, rethink your *yes* response because it may not be your best possible and most honest answer.

## THE POWER OF NO SELF-ASSESSMENT: *YES* WORDS

In Chapters 5 and 6 we revisited the self-assessment statements from Chapter 1. The following seven items are the *yes* statements from the Power of No Self-Assessment, with the numbers matching the assessment item numbers. These statements are not as clear as they could be. So, following each item, you'll see how the statement could be a made into a clear *yes* statement.

3. My schedule is full right now, try me in a few months.—My schedule is full right now, so *yes*, I'll work with you in three months.

4. I could do that if you can't find anyone else.—Yes, I'll help you if you don't find anyone else.

9. I'm willing to serve.—Yes, I will serve.

12. I could probably help out.—Yes, I can help out. I'll check my calendar to confirm when I can help.

15. I'd be happy to.—Yes, I'd be happy to.

18. How can I help?—Yes, I'll help. How can I help?

21. Yes.—Yes.

## POWER PRACTICE: CLARIFY YOUR *YES* STATEMENTS

1. What words do you use to say *yes*? Write them down here.

2. Circle your clear *yes* statements.

3. Now, rewrite the statements that don't clearly say *yes* so that there is no confusion about whether you are saying *yes*.

## THE BOTTOM LINE

While *yes* may be easier to say than *no*, the overuse of *yes* is just as difficult to overcome as the overuse of *no*. You now have discussion and decision tools to become a Master of No. Stop waffling, be decisive, and follow through.

## POWER SUMMARY

1. Gather your self-confidence and trust yourself to make a good decision.

2. Use the Power of No Model to have discussions that allow you to gather information and make a good decision.

3. Be sure you have an internal / external match. If you don't, be sure you are okay with that and move on.

4. Choose the words you'll use to say *yes*.

5. Say the words out loud.

6. Keep your resolve and follow through.

## CHAPTER 8

# Decision-Making Practice

## MAKING DAILY DECISIONS

Because every day life moves so quickly, you may feel overwhelmed when faced with a person needing an answer from you. The pressures of time, people, projects, carpooling, commuting, volunteering, and finding personal time can distract you from making the best possible decisions. Despite the boxing-in that can lead you to believe that you don't have a choice, you always have a choice. Moment by moment you have a choice. Despite the distractions, the demands, the pleas, the cries, the invitations, the requests, and the promises of each day, you have the power to stop, breathe, and make a choice.

True, occasionally a real life-and-death crisis arises. Even in crisis, you can take a breath as you begin making choices about the best possible action to take. No matter what, you have choices. Every chapter so far has provided practice opportunities for preparing yourself for daily decisions, including crises. This chapter provides practice opportunities for applying the Power of No Model. The additional practice scenarios in this chapter give you an opportunity to make choices without pressure. The practices will also help you discover the actual words you will feel comfortable saying when you are ready to stop saying *maybe*, stop Yes-ism, and start better saying *no*.

We all have different experiences of hearing *no*, saying *no*, and having to follow through and stick to our *no*'s. If you've had a frustrating or punishing set of experiences, you might avoid saying *no* more often than not. Build on your experiences to create new Master of No skills. In the safety of the no-pressure pages of practice that follow, learn to use the models, approaches, and strategies that will help you refine your Master of No skills.

## POWER PRACTICE: FINDING THE WORDS TO SAY *NO*

Turn the following sentences into *no, not ever* statements. Potential answers for the skill-building Power Practices in this chapter follow each Power Practice.

| *Waffler and Yes-ism Responses* | *"No, not ever" Responses* |
| --- | --- |
| I'm not the best person for the job. | |
| Okay. | |
| We don't have the budget for that. | |
| Could we wait on that? | |
| We don't have the authority to do that. | |
| Can't you find someone else to do that? | |
| We'll see. | |
| Add that to the list. | |
| I'd like to. | |
| I'll get to it. | |
| You don't really want me to do that. | |
| I can probably help. | |
| I think I'm available. | |

| I'm going to check my schedule. | |
| --- | --- |
| I'd like to do that but . . . | |
| Sure. | |
| Yes? | |

*Potential Answers*

These are potential answers (Your answers are just as strong, as long as *no* was your first word in every response.):

I'm not the best person for the job. "No, I'm not the best person for the job. I recommend _____."

Okay. "No."

We don't have the budget for that. "No, we don't have and won't get the budget for that."

Could we wait on that? "No, we'll wait on making that purchase."

We don't have the authority to do that. "No, we don't have authorization, so we are not doing it."

Can't you find someone else to do that? "No, I'm not going to do that."

We'll see. "No, I've made my decision."

Add that to the list. "No, that is not a high priority item for us to focus on. Don't add it to the list."

I'd like to. "No thank you."

I'll get to it. "No, I won't get to it."

You don't really want me to do that. "No, I won't do that."

I can probably help. "No, I won't be able to help out."

I think I'm available. "No, I'm not available that day."

I'm going to check my schedule. "No, I'm not available that day."

I'd like to do that but . . . "No, I'm not going to join you."

Sure. "No thank you."

Yes? "No."

## POWER PRACTICE: FINDING THE WORDS TO MOVE FROM *NO* TO *MAYBE* OR *YES*

Heading the other direction, now turn the *no, never* into *no, maybe,* and then into *no now, yes later*. The reason for this exercise is that when you can comfortably convert *maybe*'s into *yes* and *no* responses, and turn *no* statements into *maybe* and *yes* statements, then you are on your way to becoming a Master of No. The first line shows an example.

| *No, never* | *No, maybe* | *No now, yes later* |
| --- | --- | --- |
| No. | Maybe? | Not now, I'll do it later. |
| No, you are not going to do that. | | |
| No, I'm not going to the store. | | |
| No, we are not going to the movie. | | |
| No, we don't have the budget. | | |
| No, we don't have staff hours available. | | |
| No, we're not buying you a car. | | |
| No, you're not spending all that. | | |
| No, I'm not completing your assignment. | | |
| No, the package hasn't arrived. | | |
| No. | | |

*Potential Answers*

Following are potential answers. See how yours compare.

| No, never | No, maybe | No now, yes later |
|---|---|---|
| No. | Maybe? | Not now. I'll do it later. |
| No, you are not going to do that. | You're not doing that are you? | Yes, you may do that. |
| No, I'm not going to the store. | I'm not sure when I'll go to the store. | I'm going to the store at 4 P.M. |
| No, we are not going to the movie. | Maybe we'll go to a movie. | Yes, we're going to the movie at 7:45 p.m. |
| No, we don't have the budget. | Maybe we can find the money. | Yes, we do have the budget. |
| No, we don't have staff hours available. | Maybe we can find staff to help. | Yes, we'll find staff hours to get this done. |
| No, we're not buying you a car. | We'll see. | Yes, we'll pay $3000 for a car. |
| No, you're not spending all that. | Maybe you can spend some of that. | Yes, you can spend $100. |
| No, I'm not completing your assignment | Maybe I'll get it done for you. | Yes, I'll complete it. |
| No, the package hasn't arrived | I don't know. | Yes, the package came an hour ago. |
| No. | Maybe. | Yes. |

## POWER PRACTICE REVISITED: SAYING *NO* OUT LOUD

You saw this activity in an earlier chapter. How has your practice been going? Take a moment to practice again. How much stronger is your *no* now than it was the first time you did this exercise?

Say *no* out loud. Right now, say NO. If you didn't just find yourself saying *no* out loud this time and with meaning, here are some questions to help you practice saying *no* out loud and with meaning. Remember, if you can't say *no* when no one is listening, how will you confidently say *no* when someone *is* listening? Respond as quickly as possible to each of the following questions. Say your answers out loud!

1. Do you want to work 100 hours a week every week?
2. Do you want to get paid less than you are worth?
3. Do you want someone to permanently take your kids, so that you'd never see them again?
4. Do you want to eat until you explode?
5. Do you want to be involved in a fatal car accident?

Now, practice saying *no* in front of a mirror.

1. With your eyes closed and without saying a word out loud, practice saying *no* silently, in your mind. Say *no* to yourself silently five times.
2. Now, with your eyes open, say *no* five times to yourself.
3. Next, with your eyes closed, say *no* out loud five times.
4. Finally, with your eyes open, say *no* out loud five times.
5. Say *no* out loud in five different tones of voice.
6. Say *no* out loud with five different facial expressions.

## POWER PRACTICE: COUNT THE TIMES

1. How many times a day do you have an opportunity to say *no*? (You don't have to actually say it out loud every time.)
2. How many times a week do you have opportunities to say *no*?
3. Where do you feel most comfortable saying *no*? At work, at home, or in the community?

## POWER SCENARIO PRACTICES: TOOL REVIEW

In this Power of No refresher (Chapter 2), what questions could you ask to apply the Power of No Model?

**P**urpose
**O**ptions and Resources
**W**hen
**E**motional Ties
**R**ights and Responsibilities.

In each of the following sixteen situations, put yourself in the place of the person who needs to say *no*. Write down how you would say *no*, or *yes*, as a Master of No. Use the five Power of No questions to determine how you would handle each situation that follows. Also write down the words and questions you would use if you found yourself in each situation.

## Work Situation 1

You've been working for your company for three years. You want a promotion and have been promised a raise that you haven't seen. Two co-workers have left and no one is being hired to take their places. Your boss comes to you and asks for help on a project that has a deadline ten days from now. The deadline would be realistic if half of your workload didn't exist.

> What will you say to your boss?
> How will you arrive at what you will say? How will you apply the
>     Power of No Model?
> How will you feel about your response?
> How will you own your response?
> If you had to create each of these three responses, how would you tell
>     your boss—
>     No, not ever:
>     No, maybe:
>     No, not now, yes later:

**Potential Answers.** In each of these situations there are no "right" answers. Potential responses are given only for the first situation in each group (Work, Home, Friends, and Community) so that you have an idea for the pattern of your responses to the rest of the situations.

**Potential Answers for Work Situation 1**

• *How will you arrive at what you will say?* By using the Power of *No* Model. Because the stated *When* of the POWER model is a timeline of ten days from now, in order to determine how realistic the request is, you can ask the boss: "What do you need the finished project to include? What resources are available to help get this done? What are my rights if I say *no*? What are my responsibilities if I say *yes*?" And internally, you'll ask yourself, "How do I really feel about this? Am I committed?"

- *How will you own your response?* You've said whatever you decided to say. So own it, don't regret it, and keep moving forward making the next decision that comes along even better than the one you've just made.

- *If you had to create each of these three responses, how would you tell your boss:*
  *No, not ever:* "No. I'm not going to do that."
  *No, maybe:* "I'll see if I can work that in."
  *No, not now, yes later:* "I'll do that next week and still meet the 10 day deadline."

## Work Situation 2

Your supervisor has just asked you to fill in for a driver. A delivery must be made by 2 P.M. to a client. And a payment is to be picked up from a second client on the return trip at 2:45 P.M. A company vehicle is not available. Your insurance doesn't cover you driving your vehicle for work-related deliveries. And, you are not bonded to handle money for your company.

> What will you say to your supervisor?
> How will you arrive at what you will say? How will you apply the
>     Power of No Model?
> How will you feel about your response?
> How will you own your response?
> If you had to create each of these three responses, how would you tell
>     your supervisor:
>     No, not ever:
>     No, maybe:
>     No, not now, yes later:

## Work Situation 3

Your organization has just been told to "cut expenses" because profits are down. How will you determine what to do?

> How will you arrive at what you will say? How will you apply the
>     Power of No Model?
> How will you feel about your response?
> How will you own your response and commitment to action?
> If you had to create each of these three responses, how would you tell
>     your supervisor:

No, not ever:
No, maybe:
No, not now, yes later:

## Work Situation 4

Your company has a policy against manager-employee relationships. You've just discovered that a manager and one of his direct reports are having a personal relationship that has also begun to negatively affect workplace productivity. Internally, you and others are frustrated about what's going on and you want the against-policy relationship to come to an end and stop affecting everyone at work. Put yourself in whatever position you currently hold at work. What will you do?

> What will you say? And to whom will you say it?
> How will you arrive at what you will say? How will you apply the
> Power of *No* Model?
> How will you feel about your say-no actions and response?
> How will you own your response?

## Work Situation 5

Describe your most frustrating say-no situation at work.

> Knowing what you now know, what will you say next time?
> How will you arrive at what you will say? How will you apply the
> Power of No Model?
> How will you feel about your response?
> How will you own your response?
> If you had to create each of these three responses, how would you tell
> your boss—
> No, not ever:
> No, maybe:
> No, not now, yes later:

## Home Situation 1

You're getting married in four months but you and your soon-to-be-spouse haven't talked about whether you'll have children or about how

many children you want to have. You don't want to have children but
you haven't figured out how to say so.

What will you say to your soon-to-be spouse?
How will you arrive at what you will say? How will you apply the
    Power of No Model?
How will you handle your spouse's response?
How will you own your response?

**Potential Answers for Home Situation 1**

- *What will you say to your soon-to-be-wed spouse?*
  Begin with the Power of No model and build a statement that you can
  share in a conversation about having children. For example:
  **P**urpose: "We haven't yet talked about having children and I'd like to
  talk about it.
  **O**ptions: "I've known since high school that I didn't want to have children. I still don't want to have children. What are your feelings about
  having children?"
  **W**hen: "I know this is hard to talk about, but I think we should really
  have this discussion before we get married."
  **E**motional Ties: "I feel strongly about this and I'm not going to change
  my mind. I don't want to have children."
  **R**ights and Responsibilities: "I've been honest with you. Please be honest
  with me. Given how I feel about having children, do you still want to
  marry me?"

- *How will you own your response?* You've said whatever you decided to
  say. So own it, don't regret it, and keep moving forward making the
  next decision that comes along even better than the one you've just
  made. Also, think about how you'll honor the commitment to your
  spouse about the number of kids you want to have.

## Home Situation 2

You've been working long hours. Your spouse has been working long
hours too. House- and yard-work that both of you used to keep up with
is not getting done. You've been avoiding a conversation about what can
change so that your family is not living in a dirty house that *no* longer
feels like home. You're exhausted and frustrated. You want everyone in
the house to feel less stressed about all of the chores needing to get done.

How will you say "enough, no more of this!"
What will you say to your spouse?
How will you arrive at what you will say? How will you apply the
 Power of No Model?
How will you handle your spouse's response?
How will you own your response?

## Home Situation 3

You've been in your house for five years and are outgrowing the space
because now there are five of you living in it. You can afford to move but
you really like the neighborhood and the schools where you live now.
Your spouse says, "I think it's time to move." Now what?

What will you say to your spouse?
How will you arrive at what you will say? How will you apply the
 Power of *No* Model?
How will you handle your spouse's response?
How will you own your response?

## Home Situation 4

Describe your most frustrating say-no situation at home.

Knowing what you now know, what will you say next time?
How will you arrive at what you will say? How will you apply the
 Power of No Model?
How will you feel about your response?
How will you own your response?
If you had to create each of these three responses, how would you say:
 No, not ever:
 No, maybe:
 No, not now, yes later:

## Friends or Extended Family Situation 1

A friend you haven't seen in years is in town. He's just called to see if
you'll go out for a beer tonight. Your spouse and kids are expecting you
home for dinner.

What will you say to your friend?

What will you say to your spouse and kids?

How will you arrive at what you will say? How will you apply the
  Power of No Model?

How will you feel about your response?

How will you own your response?

If you had to create each of these three responses, how would you tell
  your spouse:
  No, not ever:
  No, maybe:
  No, not now, yes later:

## Potential Answers for Friends or Extended Family Situation 1

- *What will you say to your friend?* Your choice: whatever you want to say.

- *What will you say to your spouse and kids?* Your choice: whatever you
  want to say.

- *How will you arrive at what you will say? How will you apply the Power
  of No Model?* Apply the Power of No Model as follows:
  **P***urpose*: Why does your friend want to get together? Does the purpose
  affect your options?
  **O***ptions*: Can you meet your friend somewhere other than at home?
  Can you invite your friend home for dinner and to meet your family?
  Can you meet after dinner with your family? Can you meet before din-
  ner with your family?
  **W***hen*: Is tonight really the only time that your friend can meet? Revisit
  your options questions to settle on a time that works for both of you.
  **E***motional Ties*: How do you feel about getting together with this friend?
  Do you want to at all, for a limited amount of time with your family,
  or without your family?
  **R***ights and Responsibilities*: You are expected at home for dinner, so
  what decision will you work out with your friend and your family so
  that everyone feels good about your decision—including you.

- *How will you own your response?* You've said whatever you decided to
  say. So own it, don't regret it, and keep moving forward making the
  next decision that comes along even better than the one you've just
  made.

- If you had to create each of these three responses, how would you tell
  your friend:
  *No, not ever*: "No, and don't call me the next time you are in town."

*No, maybe:* "I'm not sure, I'll check in at home."
*No, not now, yes later:* "I've made other commitments. Please call me before you come into town next time so that we can schedule something."

### Friends or Extended Family Situation 2

The annual high-school reunion is more stressful than it is fun for you. This year, you've reached your breaking-point: You don't want to go.

> What will you say? To whom?
> How will you arrive at what you will say? How will you apply the
>     Power of No Model?
> How will you feel about your responses?
> How will you own your response?
> If you had to create each of these three responses, how would you tell
>     your family:
> No, not ever:
> No, maybe:
> No, not now, yes later:

### Friends or Extended Family Situation 3

Your friend (or sister, brother, daughter, or son) has just dropped by asking you if you can watch the kids for a few hours—starting right now.

> How will you arrive at what you will say? How will you apply the
>     Power of No Model?
> What will you say?
> How will you feel about your response?
> How will you own your response?
> If you had to create each of these three responses, how would you say:
> No, not ever:
> No, maybe:
> No, not now, yes later:

### Friends or Extended Family Situation 4

A high-school acquaintance has called to see if, during an upcoming visit to your city, she can stay at your house for a few nights.

How will you arrive at what you will say? How will you apply the
   Power of No Model?
What will you say to your acquaintance? And what will you say to the
   people who live with you?
How will you feel about your response?
How will you own your response?
If you had to create each of these three responses, how would you say:
   No, not ever:
   No, maybe:
   No, not now, yes later:

## Community Situation 1

You've been driving your car for a year as part of a carpool to work (or
to kid's events). Two of the carpoolers have paid for their share of the gas
and parking on a monthly basis. The third person hasn't paid, nor even
discussed paying you for the last four months. Your patience is gone.
How will you say "no more."

What will you say to your carpool friend? How will you arrive at what
   you will say? How will you apply the Power of No Model?
How will you feel about your response?
How will you own your response?
If you had to create each of these three responses, how would you tell
   your carpooler:
   No, not ever:
   No, maybe:
   No, not now, yes later:

### Potential Answers for Community Situation 1

• *What will you say to your carpool friend?* Your choice: whatever you
  wanted to say.

• *How will you arrive at what you will say? How will you apply the Power
  of No Model?* Apply the Power of No Model as follows:
  **P**urpose: You want to express your frustration and bring justice and
  fairness to the situation.
  **O**ptions: Don't say anything and stay mad. Talk to the carpooling friend
  alone and find out what is going on. Talk to the carpooling friend and
  spouse over dinner with your spouse and offer to help. Talk to the
  others in the carpool, or other friends, to see if there is some challenge
  that the carpooler needs help with.

**W**hen: The longer you wait, the more everyone suffers. So, pick a time where a focused and supportive conversation can happen.

**E**motional Ties: You are already bothered, so it is time to take action.

**R**ights and Responsibilities: Everyone made an agreement to pay you for carpooling, so everyone needs to pay. You have the right and the responsibility for holding everyone to the agreement.

- *How will you own your response?* You've said whatever you decided to say. So own it, don't regret it, and keep moving forward making the next decision that comes along even better than the one you've just made. If you decide to let the carpooler keep riding without paying, how will you feel? How will the other carpoolers feel? What is really the most kind, fair, and honest response?

- If you had to create each of these three responses, how would you tell your carpooler:

  *No, not ever*: "No more. This is not fair to any of us. Please pay me by the fifteenth of this month for the whole of five months."

  *No, maybe*: "Can we work out a payment plan so that you can catch up on payments?"

  *No*, not now, *yes* later: "I understand things are tight. Can you pay me something now and we'll work out a payment plan so that you can get caught up?"

### Community Situation 2

"Please, will you chair the special events committee this year?" You already serve on a trade association committee and coach soccer for your youngest child. You believe in the new organization and would like to help. Yet you don't feel that this is the year to agree to chair a committee that you've never served on.

> What will you say to the volunteer requesting you to volunteer and serve as the chair?
> How will you arrive at what you will say? How will you apply the Power of No Model?
> How will you feel about your response?
> How will you own your response?
> If you had to create each of these three responses, how would you say:
>> No, not ever:
>> No, maybe:
>> No, not now, yes later:

## Community Situation 3

Describe your most frustrating say-no situation when interacting in the community.

> Knowing what you now know, what will you say next time?
> How will you arrive at what you will say? How will you apply the Power of No Model?
> How will you feel about your response?
> How will you own your response?
> If you had to create each of these three responses, how would you say:
> No, not ever:
> No, maybe:
> No, not now, yes later:

# POWER PRACTICE: NO-CONSEQUENCES MODEL

The consequences of saying *no* can affect your decision to say *no*. For each of the following statements and situations, write down what consequences you would consider before moving on with your conversation or with other activities.

1. As a Master of No, you've just said *No.*
   Positive Consequences:
   Negative Consequences:
   Neutral Consequences:

2. As a Master of No, you've just reflected for about ten minutes on your response to a request and have decided to say *no.*
   Positive Consequences:
   Negative Consequences:
   Neutral Consequences:

3. You're a Waffler and have just slowly said "No . . . ?"
   Positive Consequences:
   Negative Consequences:
   Neutral Consequences:

4. Yes-ism is your comfort zone and you've just said, "Yes, I'll help you. I don't know how, but I will."
   Positive Consequences:
   Negative Consequences:
   Neutral Consequences:

5. "No. I won't do that and I can't believe that you are even asking me to consider it." (Was this said by a Master of No, Waffler, or a Yes-ism person?)
Positive Consequences:
Negative Consequences:
Neutral Consequences:

6. "I'd like to help, I'm not sure when I can start." (Was this said by a Master of No, Waffler or a Yes-ism person?)
Positive Consequences:
Negative Consequences:
Neutral Consequences:

7. "You mentioned the party at work today, so I decided to come." (Was this said by a Master of No, Waffler, or a Yes-ism person?
Positive Consequences:
Negative Consequences:
Neutral Consequences:

8. "Yes, I can help out on that committee for one year, beginning July 1." (Was this said by a Master of No, Waffler or a Yes-ism person?)
Positive Consequences:
Negative Consequences:
Neutral Consequences:

## Potential Answers

For each of the following statements, consider and write down the potential consequences of having said these words out loud. These are only potential answers.

1. As a Master of No, you've just said "No."
Positive Consequences: Everyone knows you meant *no*.
Negative Consequences: Some people heard your *no* as edgy and inconsiderate.
Neutral Consequences: Everyone is clear and *no* one is put off.

2. As an Apprentice of No, you've just reflected for about ten minutes on your response of "no."
Positive Consequences: You've made a clear decision. Wafflers, Yes-ism persons, and some Apprentices appreciate seeing your decision-making process in action.
Negative Consequences: Masters of *No* thought you took too long to decide.

Neutral Consequences: Everyone is clear and *no* one is put off.

3. You're a Waffler and have just slowly said, "No . . . ?"
   Positive Consequences: You've delayed making a decision.
   Negative Consequences: You've delayed making a decision.
   Neutral Consequences: Making a decision wasn't critical, so *no* other consequences occurred.

4. *Yes*-ism is your comfort zone and you've just said, "Yes, I'll help you. I don't know how, but I will."
   Positive Consequences: You're seen as someone willing to help.
   Negative Consequences: You don't get it done and people are disappointed.
   Neutral Consequences: Not sure there are any on this one. You made a commitment to help, so if you did it people are glad and if you didn't people are unhappy.

5. "No. I won't do that. I can't believe that you are even asking me to consider it." (This was said by a Waffler because a Master of No would not have added the last sentence.")
   Positive Consequences: Everyone knows you won't do it.
   Negative Consequences: You are seen as a bit emotional and over-reactive.
   Neutral Consequences: Someone who would have reacted the same way is okay with your response.

6. "I'd like to help, I'm not sure when I can start." (This was said by a Yes-ism person.)
   Positive Consequences: You're seen as nice and as willing to help.
   Negative Consequences: You have overcommitted once again and things aren't getting done. People are frustrated with you.
   Neutral Consequences: Everything is okay.

7. "You mentioned the party at work today, so I decided to come." (This was said by a Yes-ism person.)
   Positive Consequences: Everyone is glad to see you.
   Negative Consequences: The host feels like you've crashed the party because you didn't have a specific invitation to come to the party.
   Neutral Consequences: Everything is okay, *no* harm done, *no* bad feelings exist.

8. "Yes, I can help out on that committee for one year, beginning July 1." (This was said by a Master of No.)
   Positive Consequences: You've committed and made clear when you will start.

Negative Consequences: People are unhappy that you can't start sooner.

Neutral Consequences: Everything is okay and acceptable.

(NOTE: A Yes-ism person might have said "yes," "sure," or "I can help out," and then not followed through to the degree hoped for.

## POWER PRACTICE: **YOUR POLICY OF NO**

In Chapters 4 and 5, you began recording the decisions you can make once and turn into your Policy of *No* statements. Your Policy of *No* comes from what you believe is good or bad, right or wrong, healthy and safe, or unhealthy and dangerous. It also comes from what is important to you.

1. Record your complete list of Policy of *No* statements here.

**NO!**

## My Policy of *No*

_____ (Your Signature)

_____ (Today's Date)

I will use the following values and policies to guide my decisions.

1.

2.

3.

4.

5.

6.

7.

8.

9.

10.

**My Policy of No**

*Sample Policy for an Adult*

I will use the following values and policies to guide my decisions.

1. I will only work somewhere as long as I'm having fun.

2. I will follow through on the things I commit to.

3. I will only work for someone I respect.

4. I will only buy a house that meets my needs.

5. I will only buy clothes that I like to wear and feel good in.

6. I put my family first.

7. I will take care of myself and my health.

8. I want to take at least one, one-week vacation a year.

9. I won't have unprotected sex.

10. I won't let others talk me into things that I don't believe in.

2. Coach your kids, a coworker, or a friend to also create a Policy of No statement list.

## My Policy of No

_____ (Your Signature)

_____ (Today's Date)

I will use the following values and policies to guide my decisions.

1.

2.

3.

4.

5.

6.

7.

8.

9.

10.

## My Policy of No

*Sample Policy for a Teenager*

I will use the following values and policies to guide my decisions.

1. I will study hard and get good grades.

2. I will follow through on the things I commit to.

3. I will have friends that are respectful of me and of other people.

4. I will listen to mom and dad when they're just trying to protect me.

5. I will be honest.

6. I will be kind to my friends.

7. I will be nice to my brother and sister.

8. I will buy clothes that fit, look good, and are a good value.

9. I will ask for permission to use the car.

10. I will help out around the house.

## THE BOTTOM LINE

Say *no* when you know you won't be able to do something at all. Say *no* when you know you won't be able to follow through and deliver what is requested. Ask questions, have a discussion. Remember that having information gives you power to decide. Determine what to say by using the Power of No Model, answering *yes* or *no* to the questions below:

**P**urpose: Do I understand the purpose?
**O**ptions and Resources: Have I been given options? Do I need them?
**W**hen: Can I deliver on the requested deadline?
**E**motional Ties: Do I feel good about taking this on?
**R**ights and Responsibilities: Are my rights being respected?

As discussed in Chapter 7, if you end up with more *yes* answers to these questions, *yes* might be the best answer or response. And from Chapter 5, if you end up with more *no* answers to these questions, then *no* is the best response. Make your best possible decision.

## POWER SUMMARY

1. Revisit The Power of No Self-Assessment.

2. Use your new decision-making tools every day, every time there's a decision to be made.

3. The Power of No Model.

4. The no-consequences Model.

5. Say-no personality recognition.

6. Waffler-types recognition.

7. Policy of No statements.

8. Make your *yes* mean *yes* and your *no* mean *no*.

9. Become a Master of No.

## CHAPTER 9

# More Practice Saying No

## Final Practice Scenarios

> ### POWER PREVIEW POINTS
>
> 1. Practice putting the Power of No Model into action.
>
> 2. Keep practicing here, without someone urging you to make a decision.
>
> 3. Confirm your Master of No skills.

**H**ere are nearly fifty more opportunities to practice saying *no*! How will you say *no* in each of the situations that follow?

As you think about how you'd respond to each statement, consider your internal reaction and external response. Identify which models from this book you'll apply. Identify what consequences you will consider. List what question you will ask. And write down the actual words you would use to say *no*. Do these practices for real. "No" is a complete sentence but it rarely has the finesse you need to maintain a relationship with the person you are talking to. And only rarely is it okay to destroy a relationship with someone.

*Directions:* Answer the first three questions for each situation so that in the fourth question you can write down how you would actually say *no* out loud in each situation.

1. A relative is forcing a third helping of dinner on you.
   a. How will you apply the Power of No Model? In other words, what questions will you ask yourself or others?

   b. What consequences will you consider?

   c. What say-no personality will you use?

   d. What words will you use to say *no* to your relative?

2. Your boss wants you to lie on your timecard by punching out and then continuing to work for another hour.
   a. How will you apply the Power of No Model? In other words, what questions will you ask yourself or others?
   b. What consequences will you consider?
   c. What say-no personality will you use?
   d. What words will you use to create your external *no* and to say *no* to your boss?

3. Your kids want to buy something that you think is inappropriate to give as a birthday present.
   a. How will you apply the Power of No Model? In other words, what questions will you ask yourself or others?
   b. What consequences will you consider?
   c. What say-no personality will you use?
   d. What words will you use to create your external *no* and to say *no* to your child?

4. The noise around your workspace has gotten so distracting that you aren't getting anything done.
   a. How will you apply the Power of No Model? In other words, what questions will you ask yourself or others?
   b. What consequences will you consider?
   c. What say-no personality will you use?
   d. What words will you use to create your external *no* and to say *no* to your coworkers?

5. Your doctor wants you to take a medicine whose side effects you don't like.
   a. How will you apply the Power of No Model? In other words, what questions will you ask yourself or others?
   b. What consequences will you consider?
   c. What say-no personality will you use?
   d. What words will you use to create your external *no* and to say *no* to your doctor?

6. Your youngest child is having a temper-tantrum in the store. You're not even sure what the tantrum is about.
   a. How will you apply the Power of No Model? In other words, what questions will you ask yourself or others?

     b. What consequences will you consider?

     c. What say-no personality will you use?

     d. What words will you use to create your external *no* and to say *no* to your little tantrum child?

7. Your teenager wants to borrow the car to get to work.

     a. How will you apply the Power of No Model? In other words, what questions will you ask yourself or others?

     b. What consequences will you consider?

     c. What say-no personality will you use?

     d. What words will you use to create your external *no* and to say *no* to your teen?

8. Your teenager wants to borrow the car to go to a party.

     a. How will you apply the Power of No Model? In other words, what questions will you ask yourself or others?

     b. What consequences will you consider?

     c. What say-no personality will you use?

     d. What words will you use to create your external *no* and to say *no* to your teen?

9. Your daughter is eleven and she wants to start wearing make-up.

     a. How will you apply the Power of No Model? In other words, what questions will you ask yourself or others?

     b. What consequences will you consider?

     c. What say-no personality will you use?

     d. What words will you use to create your external *no* and to say *no* to your daughter?

10. Your son is fifteen and you've just found por*n*ography magazines in his room.

     a. How will you apply the Power of No Model? In other words, what questions will you ask yourself or others?

     b.  What consequences will you consider?

     c. What say-no personality will you use?

     d. What words will you use to create your external *no* and to say *no* to your son.

11. Your date is hinting about having sex. You don't plan to or want to have sex.

     a. How will you apply the Power of No Model? In other words, what questions will you ask yourself or others?

     b. What consequences will you consider?

     c. What say-no personality will you use?

d. What words will you use to create your external *no* and to say *no* to your date?

12. A coworker is offering you illegal drugs.
    a. How will you apply the Power of No Model? In other words, what questions will you ask yourself or others?
    b. What consequences will you consider?
    c. What say-no personality will you use?
    d. What words will you use create your external *no* and to say *no* to your coworker?

13. A friend is on a spending spree while you are shopping together. You are being teased to "join in on the fun and spend some money."
    a. How will you apply the Power of No Model? In other words, what questions will you ask yourself or others?
    b. What consequences will you consider?
    c. What say-no personality will you use?
    d. What words will you use to create your external *no* and to say *no* to your friend?

14. The person with whom you are in a relationship is physically hurting you.
    a. How will you apply the Power of No Model? In other words, what questions will you ask yourself or others?
    b. What consequences will you consider?
    c. What say-no personality will you use?
    d. What words will you use to create your external *no* and to say *no* to stop the pain?

15. The person with whom you are in a relationship is saying things to control your every move.
    a. How will you apply the Power of No Model? In other words, what questions will you ask yourself or others?
    b. What consequences will you consider?
    c. What say-no personality will you use?
    d. What words will you use to create your external *no* and to say *no* to the person trying to control you?

16. The person with whom you are in a relationship at least once a week says things that hurt your feelings.
    a. How will you apply the Power of No Model? In other words, what questions will you ask yourself or others?
    b. What consequences will you consider?
    c. What say-no personality will you use?
    d. What words will you use to create your external *no* and to say *no*?

17. The person you live with refuses to do any of the things you had agreed to do together.
    a. How will you apply the Power of No Model? In other words, what questions will you ask yourself or others?
    b. What consequences will you consider?
    c. What say-no personality will you use?
    d. What words will you use to create your external *no* and to say "no more" to this behavior?

18. Your boss is asking for help on another project that you don't have time for.
    a. How will you apply the Power of No Model? In other words, what questions will you ask yourself or others?
    b. What consequences will you consider?
    c. What say-no personality will you use?
    d. What words will you use to create your external *no* and to say *no* to your boss?

19. Your team is pleading for more time to complete a project.
    a. How will you apply the Power of No Model? In other words, what questions will you ask yourself or others?
    b. What consequences will you consider?
    c. What say-no personality will you use?
    d. What words will you use to create your external *no* and to say *no* to your team?

20. When you are checking out at the grocery store, the clerk asks if you'd like to donate one dollar to some cause.
    a. How will you apply the Power of No Model? In other words, what questions will you ask yourself or others?
    b. What consequences will you consider?
    c. What say-no personality will you use?
    d. What words will you use to create your external *no* and to say *no*?

21. Your income tax form asks you to check a box to donate money to one of five causes.
    a. How will you apply the Power of No Model? In other words, what questions will you ask yourself or others?
    b. What consequences will you consider?
    c. What say-no personality will you use?
    d. What words or actions will you use to create your external *no* and to say *no* on the form?

22. The waitress asks if you'd like dessert.
    a. How will you apply the Power of No Model? In other words, what questions will you ask yourself or others?

b. What consequences will you consider?

c. What say-no personality will you use?

d. What words will you use to create your external *no* and to say *no* to the waitress?

23. The fast food clerk asks "do you want to giant-size this for 39 cents more?"
    a. How will you apply the Power of No Model? In other words, what questions will you ask yourself or others?
    b. What consequences will you consider?
    c. What say-no personality will you use?
    d. What words will you use to create your external *no* and to say *no*?

24. You've called to speak to a client, and the receptionist asks "will you hold please?"
    a. How will you apply the Power of No Model? In other words, what questions will you ask yourself or others?
    b. What consequences will you consider?
    c. What say-no personality will you use?
    d. What words will you use to create your external *no* and to say *no*?

25. Your mother wants you to "come home" for the holidays.
    a. How will you apply the Power of No Model? In other words, what questions will you ask yourself or others?
    b. What consequences will you consider?
    c. What say-no personality will you use?
    d. What words will you use to create your external *no* and to say *no* to your mother?

26. Your father wants you to "get a better job."
    a. How will you apply the Power of No Model? In other words, what questions will you ask yourself or others?
    b. What consequences will you consider?
    c. What say-no personality will you use?
    d. What words will you use to create your external *no* and to say *no* to your father?

27. Your siblings want you to be the one to let your parent(s) come live with you.
    a. How will you apply the Power of No Model? In other words, what questions will you ask yourself or others?
    b. What consequences will you consider?
    c. What say-no personality will you use?
    d. What words will you use to create your external *no* and to say *no* to your siblings?

28. You're having trouble saying *no* at work but the decision at hand requires a *no*.
    a. How will you apply the Power of No Model? In other words, what questions will you ask yourself or others?
    b. What consequences will you consider?
    c. What say-no personality will you use?
    d. What words will you use to create your external *no* and to say *no*?

29. One of your employees is not performing well and is close to losing his job. You want him to turn things around so you don't have to fire him.
    a. How will you apply the Power of No Model? In other words, what questions will you ask yourself or others?
    b. What consequences will you consider?
    c. What say-no personality will you use?
    d. What words will you use to create your external *no* and to say *no* to your employee?

30. Your spouse wants to have another child and you don't.
    a. How will you apply the Power of No Model? In other words, what questions will you ask yourself or others?
    b. What consequences will you consider?
    c. What say-no personality will you use?
    d. What words will you use to create your external *no* and to say *no* to your spouse?

31. Your spouse wants to move to another city and you don't.
    a. How will you apply the Power of No Model? In other words, what questions will you ask yourself or others?
    b. What consequences will you consider?
    c. What say-no personality will you use?
    d. What words will you use to create your external *no* and to say *no* to your spouse?

32. Your daughter wants you to spend $20,000 on her wedding and you can't afford it.
    a. How will you apply the Power of No Model? In other words, what questions will you ask yourself or others?
    b. What consequences will you consider?
    c. What say-no personality will you use?
    d. What words will you use to create your external *no* and to say *no* to your daughter?

33. Your son wants you to buy him a new car for $18,000 and you can't afford it.

a. How will you apply the Power of No Model? In other words, what questions will you ask yourself or others?
b. What consequences will you consider?
c. What say-no personality will you use?
d. What words will you use to create your external *no* and to say *no* to your son?

34. Your child is afraid of monsters under the bed and in the closet.
    a. How will you apply the Power of No Model? In other words, what questions will you ask yourself or others?
    b. What consequences will you consider?
    c. What say-no personality will you use?
    d. What words will you use to create comfort for your child to go to bed?

35. You want to buy a new car. The salesman keeps talking you into upgrades. The total price is $3,000 more than you can afford to spend.
    a. How will you apply the Power of No Model? In other words, what questions will you ask yourself or others?
    b. What consequences will you consider?
    c. What say-no personality will you use?
    d. What words will you use to create your external *no* and to say *no* to the salesman?

36. The team at work has a birthday party for each employee. You don't want them to have one for you.
    a. How will you apply the Power of No Model? In other words, what questions will you ask yourself or others?
    b. What consequences will you consider?
    c. What say-no personality will you use?
    d. What words will you use to create your external *no* and to say, *no, thank you*?

37. The vendor you rely on to fill weekly orders has just announced a 15 percent price increase. Your business can't afford the increase. Other suppliers are available.
    a. How will you apply the Power of No Model? In other words, what questions will you ask yourself or others?
    b. What consequences will you consider?
    c. What say-no personality will you use?
    d. What words will you use to create your external *no* and to say *no* to the vendor?

38. One of your employees wants to go to a trade-show and conference as a part of a personal development plan for training. You don't think it is the best conference to go to.

    a. How will you apply the Power of No Model? In other words, what questions will you ask yourself or others?

    b. What consequences will you consider?

    c. What say-no personality will you use?

    d. What words will you use to create your external *no* and to say *no* to your employee?

39. You don't want to go with your friends on the annual get-together-trip next month.

    a. How will you apply the Power of No Model? In other words, what questions will you ask yourself or others?

    b. What consequences will you consider?

    c. What say-no personality will you use?

    d. What words will you use to create your external *no* and to say *no* to your friends?

40. Your neighbor (or coworker, boss, friend, or sibling) keeps asking to borrow things and then doesn't return them. You are tired of it.

    a. How will you apply the Power of No Model? In other words, what questions will you ask yourself or others?

    b. What consequences will you consider?

    c. What say-no personality will you use?

    d. What words will you use to create your external *no* and to say *no*?

41. You find yourself failing to make a decision about letting your daughter sleep over at a friend's house for three nights. You know that you want and need to say *no*. Consider your emotional ties a message of safety for your daughter.

    a. How will you apply the Power of No Model? In other words, what questions will you ask yourself or others?

    b. What consequences will you consider?

    c. What say-no personality will you use?

    d. What words will you use to create your external *no* and to say *no*?

42. You are stalling on a decision about whether to serve on a volunteer board. You believe in the cause, yet are doing too many things now.

    a. How will you apply the Power of No Model? In other words, what questions will you ask yourself or others?

    b. What consequences will you consider?

    c. What say-no personality will you use?

    d. What words will you use to create your external *no* and to say *no*?

43. You are delaying a conversation with your parents. You need to say *no* to their request to let your kids spend the summer with them.

    a. How will you apply the Power of No Model? In other words, what questions will you ask yourself or others?

    b. What consequences will you consider?

    c. What say-no personality will you use?

    d. What words will you use to create your external *no* and to say *no* to your parents.

44. Someone is standing too close to you.

    a. How will you apply the Power of No Model? In other words, what questions will you ask yourself or others?

    b. What consequences will you consider?

    c. What say-no personality will you use?

    d. What words will you use to create your external *no* and to say *no* to the invasion of your space?

45. Someone is touching you in a way that you don't like.

    a. How will you apply the Power of No Model? In other words, what questions will you ask yourself or others?

    b.  What consequences will you consider?

    c. What say-no personality will you use?

    d. What words will you use to create your external *no* and to say *no* to this unwanted contact?

46. Your children are fighting.

    a. How will you apply the Power of No Model? In other words, what questions will you ask yourself or others?

    b. What consequences will you consider?

    c. What say-no personality will you use?

    d. What words will you use to create your external *no* and to say *no* to your children?

47. Your coworkers are fighting.

    a. How will you apply the Power of No Model? In other words, what questions will you ask yourself or others?

    b. What consequences will you consider?

    c. What say-no personality will you use?

    d. What words will you use to create your external *no* and to say *no* to your coworkers?

48. You have a customer that you no longer want or can afford to do business with. It's time to fire the customer.

    a. How will you apply the Power of No Model? In other words, what questions will you ask yourself or others?

    b. What consequences will you consider?

c. What say-no personality will you use?
d. What words will you use to create your external *no* and to say "stop" to your customers?

Consider what Dave Lakhani, president of Bold Approach, Inc., a marketing and business optimization firm, has to say. "Every business actually reaches a stage where the difficult decision to let a client go must be wrestled with. As business people we've development a desire to service the customer *no* matter what their demands, *no* matter how uncooperative they are, and *no* matter how draining it is on staff or resources. The truth of the matter is that there are a few clients who deserve to be fired."

49. You enjoy volunteering for good causes in your community. Right now you serve on two committees for your children's school and coach a soccer team. You also serve on one non-profit board in your community. Now, someone you've known for fifteen years is asking you to serve on a new board for their new non-profit.
a. How will you apply the Power of No Model? In other words, what questions will you ask yourself or others?
b. What consequences will you consider?
c. What say-no personality will you use?
d. What words will you use to create your external *no*?

50. What is your favorite way to say *no*?

What do you like about it? What do you sound like, look like, and feel like when you say this *no* to others?

## Potential Answers

Here follow potential answers for the first ten scenarios. There are no "right" answers because each of us brings different experiences and additional meaning to each of these generic situations. View these as idea-starters to help you complete the remaining list of situations.

1. A relative is forcing a third helping of dinner on you.
a. How will you apply the Power of No Model? In other words, what questions will you ask yourself or others?
**P**urpose: She wants to feel that you like her cooking.
**O**ptions: Politely decline the third helping and compliment her cooking. Ask to take some home for dinner tomorrow.
**W**hen: Now before the third helping is on your plate.
**E**motional Ties: Stop feeling like a victim and stand up for yourself.
**R**ights: You have a right to say "no, thank you."

b. *What consequences will you consider?* Hurting her feelings.

c. *What say-no personality will you use?* Gracious and Detailed.

d. *What words will you use to say no to your relative?* "No, thank you. It was a delicious dinner and I'm very full. I had two helpings already."

2. Your boss wants you to lie on your timecard by punching out and then continuing to work for another hour.

a. *How will you apply the Power of No Model? In other words, what questions will you ask yourself or others?* With your Policy of No statement. Ask: "Isn't there a budget for overtime?"

b. *What consequences will you consider?* Losing my job.

c. *What say-no personality will you use?* Direct.

d. *What words will you use to create your external no and to say no to your boss?* "No."

3. Your kids want to buy something that you think is inappropriate to give as a birthday present.

a. *How will you apply the Power of No Model? In other words, what questions will you ask yourself or others?* Coach the child through a Power of No conversation with a series of questions that are age-appropriate. Questions you could ask: "Why do you want to get that gift? Do you think it is appropriate?"

b. *What consequences will you consider?* Making the child unhappy. Buying the gift and embarrassing yourself with the other parents.

c. *What say-no personality will you use?* Direct, Inspirational.

d. *What words will you use to create your external no and to say no to your child?* After coaching the child through the Power of No questions, he may decide on a different gift. Or, he may decide that is the gift he intends to get and you will say "No. Pick something else to buy."

4. The noise around your workspace has gotten so distracting that you aren't getting anything done.

a. *How will you apply the Power of No Model? In other words, what questions will you ask yourself or others?*

**P**urpose: You need quiet in order to work.

**O**ptions: Move to another location. Talk to co-workers. Work from home one day. You could ask: "Is there another place you can finish the conversation?"

**W**hen: Take action today.

**E**motional Ties: Your emotions are *now* also contributing to your inability to get work done.

**R**ights: You have a right to a quiet workspace, or a sound protected work area.

   b. *What consequences will you consider?* Making others unhappy with me. Realizing that others may be distracted too and be happy that I've said something!

   c. *What say-no personality will you use?* Direct, Gracious.

   d. *What words will you use to create your external no and to say no to your coworkers?* "It's getting very *noisy*. We can't get work with customers done, so please move your conversation somewhere else. Thanks."

5. Your doctor wants you to take a medicine whose side effects you don't like.

   a. *How will you apply the Power of No Model? In other words, what questions will you ask yourself or others?*

     **P**urpose: Your doctor wants to help. You want to feel better without the side effects that have been described.

     **O**ptions: Ask the doctor, "What are my other options? How else can I be treated?" If you don't like what the doctor says, get another opinion.

     **W**hen: Right *now*, while you are in the office.

     **E**motional Ties: You have a right to feel concerned and frustrated, so express your feelings.

     **R**ights and Responsibilities: You are responsible for your health and well-being. You have a right to protect yourself and to make choices. So, speak up and ask the doctor for other options.

   b. *What consequences will you consider?* What consequences will you consider? The other side effects. The consequences of *not* taking any medication. The consequences of getting *a*nother opinion.

   c. *What say-no personality will you use?* Direct.

   d. *What words will you use to create your external no and to say no to your doctor?* "No, I won't take that. What else is an option?"

6. Your youngest child is having a temper-tantrum in the store. You're not even sure what the tantrum is about.

   a. *How will you apply the Power of No Model? In other words, what questions will you ask yourself or others?*

     **P**urpose: Remain calm and get the child to calm down.

     **O**ptions: Stop shopping and leave the store. Hold a Time-Out for the child and stop shopping there in the store for one minute. Calmly ask: "What is it that you want?" Ignore the child and keep shopping.

     **W**hen: Handle it now.

     **E**motional Ties: Embarrassment, anger, frustration.

*Rights and Responsibilities:* You are the parent and as such you have a right and a responsibility to calm and discipline your child.

b. *What consequences will you consider?* Embarrassment. Never solving the problem.

c. *What say-no personality will you use?* Direct.

d. *What words will you use to create your external no and to say no to your little tantrum child?* "No more. We are leaving the store and going home." (Then of course, there are the things you were about to purchase that get turned in to a clerk on your way out.)

7. Your teenager wants to borrow the car to get to work.
   a. *How will you apply the Power of No Model? In other words, what questions will you ask yourself or others?*

   **P***urpose*: You want to support your teen's work behavior.

   **O***ptions*: You can drive or you can give your teen the keys to the car.

   **W***hen*: Now is the time-frame.

   **E***motional Ties:* Because you trust this child of yours, you feel comfortable loaning the car.

   **R***ights and Responsibilities:* You can talk to your teen about the responsibilities of driving safely, returning home at the agreed upon time and about any other expectations you have about the use and return of the car.

   b. *What consequences will you consider?* Whether there'll be an accident.

   c. *What say-no personality will you use?* Direct, Inspirational.

   d. *What words will you use to create your external* no *and to say* no *to your teen?* "No, you can't drive today, I'll drive you."

8. Your teenager wants to borrow the car to go to a party.
   a. *How will you apply the Power of No Model? In other words, what questions will you ask yourself or others?*

   **P***urpose*: You do not want other teens in the car. You are concerned about this use of your car.

   **O***ptions*: You could drive the kids to the party. You could have your teen ride with someone else. You could send your teen on a bicycle. You could lend the car.

   **W***hen*: Depends on when the party is. If the party is tonight, you are deciding *now*. If the party is at the end of the week, you might take a day to think about it and to discover whether the party is still even on.

   **E***motional Ties:* Trust your instinct of concern.

**R**ights and Responsibilities: You can talk to your teen about the responsibilities of going to parties, of driving safely, of returning home at the agreed upon time and about any other expectations you have about attending parties and the use of your car if you decide to lend the car. You can ask: "When will you be home? Who is going with you? Will the parents be home?"

  b. *What consequences will you consider?* Making your child upset. Putting your child into a situation that is prone to danger.
  c. *What say-no personality will you use?* Direct.
  d. *What words will you use to create your external* no *and to say* no *to your teen?* "No, not only may you not have the car, you aren't going to the party either."

9. Your daughter is eleven and she wants to start wearing make-up.
  a. *How will you apply the Power of No Model? In other words, what questions will you ask yourself or others?*
    **P**urpose: You have an opportunity to help your daughter learn to wear make-up appropriately for her age.
    **O**ptions: You can say *no*. You can say *yes* and leave her to her own activities. You can say *yes* and shop with her, show her how to apply make-up. You can ask: "Why? What does make-up do for people who wear it?"
    **W**hen: You get to pick the timing. You are the parent.
    **E**motional Ties: Depends on you!
    **R**ights and Responsibilities: Again, you are the parent, with your own values and concerns. So you get to share what your values are and what your expectations about wearing make-up are.
  b. *What consequences will you consider?* Frustrating your daughter. Having her go behind your back. Helping her understand the best ways to apply make-up.
  c. *What say-no personality will you use?* Direct, Inspirational.
  d. *What words will you use create your external* no *and to say* no *to your daughter?* "No. When you are thirteen we'll talk about this some more."

10. Your son is fifteen and you've just found pornography magazines in his room.
  a. *How will you apply the Power of No Model? In other words, what questions will you ask yourself or others?*
    **P**urpose: You want to understand why he is drawn to these magazines. You want to discover whether it is time for a discussion on the responsibilities of adult sexual behavior.

**O***ptions*: You can ignore it. You can challenge him. You can punish him. You can calmly have a conversation to get at the Purpose of his interests.

**W***hen*: You are the parent, you pick the time.

**E***motional Ties*: Whatever yours are, your son has emotional ties too. Consider both yours and his so that you can have a meaningful conversation rather than a shouting match.

**R***ights and Responsibilities*: You have your own values. This is an opportunity to share your values and to help your son develop a clear sense and ownership of his own values and attitudes.

b. *What consequences will you consider?* Is this an opportunity for education, for punishment, or for something else?

c. *What say-no personality will you use?* Direct, Gracious, Inspirational.

d. *What words will you use create your external no and to say no to your son?* "No, these magazines are not a compliment to women or to men. If you want to learn about anatomy and sex, we'll go together and learn all you want to know."

## THE BOTTOM LINE

Remember to say *no* when you know you won't be able to do something at all. Say *no* when you know you won't be able to follow through and deliver what is requested. Ask questions, have a discussion. Having information gives you power to decide. Determine what to say by using the Power of No Model and answering *yes* or *no* to the questions below.

**P***urpose*: Do I understand the purpose?
**O***ptions*: Have I been given options? Do I need them?
**W***hen*: Can I deliver on the requested deadline?
**E***motional Ties*: Do I feel good about taking this on?
**R***ights and Responsibilities*: Are my rights being respected?

When you have more *yes* answers to these questions, *yes* might be the best answer or response. When you have more *no* answers to these questions, then *no* is the best response. Make your best possible decision the first time.

## POWER SUMMARY:

1. Use your new decision-making tools every day, every time there's a decision to be made.

2. Make your *yes* mean *yes* and your *no* mean *no*.

3. Become a Master of No.

4. Keep Your Resolve.

## CHAPTER 10

# *Keeping Your Resolve*

## POWER PREVIEW POINTS

1. Use the Quick Tip guides for saying *maybe, yes,* and *no.*

2. Recognize that there is not a funny way to say *no.*

3. Become a Master of No.

How many times have you said *no,* meant *no* and then let it turn into a *yes*? That's part of the trouble. *No*'s that regularly turn into *yes* make the word *no* mean *maybe.* Workplace demands often require saying *yes.* Children having tantrums wear you down to a *yes.* And family commitments that are important to you, keep you busy. The daily demand seems to be to say *yes* a hundred times. With all the pressure to say *yes,* how can you say *no,* mean it, and stick to it?

First you can admit that you want or need to say *no.* Learn to embrace your internal *no* so that you can feel comfortable allowing yourself to make a *no* decision. Draw on your Policy of No statements for strength. Then, recognize the say-no personalities involved and apply the Power of No Model to get the information you need to say and own your *no.* Finally, choose the words you'll use to say *no* and say *no* out loud.

Okay, so it's not always that easy. This chapter provides you with several Quick Tips and strategies for keeping your resolve once you've said *no.* Some of the strategies will work for you and others won't. Concentrate on the strategies that you will use and that you believe will work for you.

# QUICK TIPS FOR SAYING *MAYBE*, *YES*, AND *NO*

Use the tools from the previous chapters and keep these Quick Tip guides at hand and in mind. These Tips are designed as quick reference reminders for saying *yes*, *no*, or *maybe*. Keep the Tip pages by your phone, take them to meetings, use them when preparing for a conversation, and when you are refreshing yourself on how to keep your resolve after you've made a decision and given your response.

After reading through all three Quick Tip guides, go back over the lists and highlight the two or three key items from each list that you'll most likely find helpful and use.

## Quick Tips for Saying No

Say *no* when:

1. The activity or request doesn't help you accomplish your goals. Therefore, it is not relevant.

2. Your time is already scheduled. Even with juggling, shifting, and rescheduling you can't find time to take on another activity. This has to do with the Priority Decision Grid discussed in Chapter 3.

3. You don't have the skill to complete the request.

4. You don't have the time to acquire the skill.

5. You don't have the energy to acquire the skill.

6. You don't have the energy to complete the task.

7. You don't like the activity and won't suffer if you say *no*.

8. You don't want to say *yes* and you won't suffer if you say *no*.

9. The consequences of saying *no* outweigh the consequences of saying *yes*.

## POWER PRACTICE: START WITH THE EASY *No's*

1. What is the easiest thing for you to say *no* to? Why?

2. Who is the easiest person for you to say *no* to? Why?

3. Do you say *no* to this activity or person every time? Why?

4. How will you be consistent with the easy *no's* and say *no* every time you need to?

*Quick Tips for Safely Saying* Maybe *and Keeping Your Resolve*

Legitimate Waffling can be acceptable. You can safely say *maybe* when:

1. More information is needed. You need more information to make a decision. And you will make the decision.

2. Some else has to decide. When someone else has to approve or authorize the decision, *maybe* is okay, as long as a decision is made. (In this case, a Waffle becomes a Legitimate Waffle because a decision is made.)

3. The consequences of saying *maybe* outweigh the consequences of saying *yes* or *no*.

---

## POWER PRACTICE: MODIFY THE *MAYBE'S*

1. What do you tend to say *maybe* to? Why?

2. What do you really want your response to be? *Yes* or *no*?

3. How will you say *no* instead of *maybe* the next time you need to say *no*?

*Quick Tips for Saying* Yes *and Keeping Your Resolve*

Say *yes* when:

1. You can help others get done what they need to get done. By doing so, you'll gain more support for getting your tasks done too. Ultimately, you'll accomplish your goal more quickly.

2. You have the time to say *yes*. You won't let other important items fall off of your to do list if you say *yes*.

3. You have the skill to say *yes*. If you've never done the task and you want or need to say *yes*, how will you gain the skill?

4. You have the energy to say *yes*. Remember, however, that being so tired that all parts of your life suffer is not a path to long-term health and success.

5. You like the activity and will rearrange other things to be able to say *yes*. None of your other commitments will suffer.

6. The consequences of saying *yes* outweigh the consequences of saying *no*.

## NO FUNNY WAY TO SAY *NO*

Let that really sink in. There is not a funny way of saying *no*. Some would argue that "what part of *no* don't you understand" is a funny way to say *no*. Tone of voice and facial expressions make a big difference in how a message is understood. "What part of *no* don't you understand" was born out of frustration and so it is really a direct say-no personality statement that is a firm and angry statement rather than a humorous statement. You've read a story from a team that created a humorous story to go with their hearing of "what part of *no* don't you understand"; however, that is the story of meaning given by that team to a statement that really isn't funny.

Any attempt I've heard at a funny way of saying *no* could be confused with harshness, rudeness, meanness, or sarcasm. In other words, the greedy say-no personality appears to be at work. Saying *no* is not about alienation and confusion. Saying *no* is meant to be an act of clarity, politeness, diplomacy, discipline, and discernment. When you say *no*, make it an honest act upon which you'll follow through.

## POWER PRACTICE: A FUNNY *NO*?

1. Think of a way of saying *no* that *you* think is funny. Is it clear? Will it offend anyone? Will everyone who hears it understand your message?

2. Can't think of a funny way to say *no*? That's fine.

3. If you have discovered a truly humorous way of saying *no*, please turn to Appendix E to share your story.

## THE BOTTOM LINE

Be clear about what you want to communicate. Make *no* mean *no*, and *yes* mean *yes*. Put the Power of No Model to work. Understand and be able to explain the *Purpose* of a request, the *Options* available for completing the task, *When* the deadline is, the *Emotions* that may attach to the completion of the task, and the *Rights and Responsibilities* that go along with saying *yes* or saying *no* to the task or request. When you aren't clear, listeners can't be clear, and *no* one can deliver a successful result when messages are not clear.

When you say "Stop waffling," you're saying that clear decisions are needed. Humor can be confusing, hurtful, or even offensive. So, save the humor for something other than saying *no* to a request. And focus on the clarity of your *yes* and *no* responses so that you can keep your resolve and not change your mind and response later.

## POWER SUMMARY

1. Just because you think you are being funny, others may not understand what you are saying.

2. Be clear with your *no* and *yes* statements so that others understand what you are saying.

3. Keep your resolve and keep moving forward.

## CHAPTER 11

# *Fifty Mantras for Saying* No

## POWER PREVIEW POINTS

1. Use these Mantras to help you keep your resolve once you've said *no*.

2. Maintain and Expand your Mastery of No.

Sometimes your head tells you *no* and your heart tells you yes. You say *no* out loud, and if you lose your resolve you find yourself saying yes. Sometimes the internal voice says *no* and you talk yourself into saying yes. So, you say *yes* out loud, only to find yourself miserable, or worse, in danger.

Once you determine that *no* is the word you wish to speak, simply say *no*. Mean it. Stick to it. Stand behind it. *No* means no. When you find yourself waffling, wavering, and wandering, keep your resolve by using one of the following strategies to say *no* and stick to it.

The following list of mantras and strategies will help you keep your resolve once you've made a decision. Circle or highlight the approaches and mantras that you plan to use the next time you need to say *no* and keep your resolve. Revisit these strategies often as you work to become a Master of No.

1. Give yourself time to think before announcing your decision. Being clear about why you've made your decision will help you keep your resolve.

2. Ask for time to think the request over. Then apply the Power of No Model to be clear about why you are saying *no*. Doing this will give you confidence in your *no* responses.

3. Take the Power of No Self-Assessment again to see how you are improving. Continue doing what works. Try a new approach to overcome the weak moments.

4. After you've said *no*, remove yourself from the situation.

5. Find an ally who will keep reminding you why you said *no* and who will help you keep saying *no*.

6. Practice with the easy things. What is most easy to say *no* to? Start there, say *no* to this thing or activity every day this week. Maybe it is easiest to say *no* to second servings of food. You could start by saying *no* to an impulse purchase at the grocery check-out. You could start by saying *no* to buying that shirt just because it is on sale.

7. Stand your ground. Literally, stand with your feet firmly on the ground, about shoulder width apart. Take a deep breath, breathe deeply, and calmly. Listen to the other person so that you can discover whether *no* is the best response. When you discover that *no* is the right thing to say, say *no*. Stay standing firm and breathing deeply until you know that your decision is understood.

8. Use the word *no* to set boundaries that protect you, your family members, friends, and other people. When you are focused on protecting the people important to you, you are more likely to keep your resolve.

9. Use the word *no* to set boundaries that protect your time, energy, and assets. Revisit Chapter 3 and the self-protection discussions.

10. Be honest. When you arrive at the best possible decision based on the information you have, *no* is an honorable and ethical response. Accepting this can help you keep your resolve.

11. Start your *no* response with the word *no*.

12. Know that *no* is rarely as popular as yes.

13. Own it as your own. No blaming, finger-pointing, or shifting responsibility to someone else. You made the decision. You've said *no*. You can support why you've said *no*. You know the consequences of saying *no*. So, accept that you said *no* and be responsible for having said it.

14. Own it. Said another way, it is your choice and right to say *no*, so own it.

15. Stop beating yourself up. Once you've said *no*, and owned it, things can go wrong or you can change your mind. Rather than being hard on yourself, make some observations. Shirlene Elledge, relationship

instructor and coach, makes this suggestion: "Rather than thinking something is wrong with your decision, notice what has worked, what could be done differently next time, and notice what you can learn from what happened this time."

16. Have faith and belief in your judgment. When you decide to say *no*, trust your decision and stand by your decision.

17. Remember ethicist David Gill's point: "The ability to say *no* shows that you do have sound judgment."

18. You do not owe anyone an explanation. You've made your decision. You know why and that's what matters.

19. Remember self-defense expert Chris Kent's statement, "*No* is a complete sentence."

20. Walk away from bad deals. When you say *no* this way, you've done so because you weren't being treated fairly. You deserve to be treated fairly. Claim your right to be treated fairly.

21. Changing a say-no habit begins with awareness. And now that you are more aware, you can better keep your resolve.

22. Keep your resolve because more often than not, it works out to be better than if you'd said what someone else wanted you to say.

23. Say *no* in writing when you find that saying *no* in person is too difficult or feels too dangerous.

24. It is sometimes a good thing to say *no* to customers, vendors, and suppliers. So, once you've decided, go for it, and be okay with saying *no* to both the people you pay and those who pay you.

25. Believe in yourself. You have a right to say *no*.

26. Consequences. Consider the consequences before you say *no* or yes, and be prepared for those or other consequences to occur. Remember that you can always ask for more information and make new decisions if things change.

27. Practice with the Power of No Model, so that the categories of POWER questions race to mind when you need them: Purpose, Options and Resources, When, Emotional Ties, and Rights and Responsibilities. Knowing that you've gathered as much information as possible before making a decision can help you keep your resolve.

28. Realize that when you model saying *no* in your life, others also learn to appropriately say yes and *no*.

29. Think for yourself. Don't go along with everyone else. You know why you are making your decision. When you go along with everyone else, it's too easy to start waffling because every time other people change their minds, you end up changing yours too.

30. Know that your *no* is in your best interest. This is not only okay, it helps you to protect yourself, your time, and your energy.

31. Consider whether your *no* is in someone else's best interest. If so, you are providing someone else protection by saying *no*.

32. Respect. Saying *no* can be a form of respect. Saying *no* can show that you have respect for yourself and for someone else.

33. Respect. Saying *no* when you aren't being treated fairly is a form of claiming your self-respect.

34. Integrity. Saying *no* when you know that you won't be able to follow through on the commitment is an ethical response.

35. Never underestimate the power of the word *no*.

36. Be clear on your intent for saying *no*. In other words, know what you want to have happen after you've said *no*.

37. Be clear about your responsibilities after you've said *no*. You don't want to get caught in a no-win situation or in a blaming game. Confirm your responsibilities after you say *no*.

38. Using the word *no* is not about power over someone else. *No* is about having control and power over your own decision making. Once you've made a decision, keep your resolve.

39. Saying *no* is not a rejection of another person. Focusing on issues will make it easier to keep your resolve.

40. Ask others for help. Find a skilled Master of No and ask for help when you feel that keeping your resolve may be difficult.

41. Say *no* out loud every time you need to. It is not enough to think *no*. Thinking it is only 50 percent of the process. Other people can't read your mind, so say *no* out loud.

42. Prevent letting your *no* become a *yes* by using the Power of No Model.

43. Ask yourself why saying *no* to children is necessary and yet why it is not okay to say *no* to adults.

44. Stop being a Waffler. Whether you are flakey-waffling or waffling, stop it. When you determine that you need to be a Legitimate Waffler, be decisive, and mean what you say.

45. Consider why you so often wait until you are angry, burdened, or too tired before you'll say *no*. Why do you do it? Now, what will you do to stop it?

46. Recall the Priority Decision Grid from Chapter 3. If an activity or request for help is not important or relevant, say *no*.

47. If the time frame of a request is unrealistic and is not negotiable, say *no*. Revisit the Priority Decision Grid in Chapter 3.

48. Find the courage to say *no* and stick to it. Children have written about their observations of courage in people who say *no*. Adults, military leaders, and religious leaders have written about the courage to say *no*. An unknown writer wrote the following words about courage for one of Pope John Paul II's speeches in 2003. The section of the speech is titled, "Courage to say *no* to cultures of death, selfishness, terrorism, and armed conflict." What struck me were the next two sentences: "This is why choices need to be made so that humanity can still have a future. Therefore, the peoples of the earth and their leaders must sometimes have the courage to say *No*."

49. Your *no* can give other the courage they need to say *no* as well.

50. Remember the power of the word *NO*!

## POWER PRACTICE: STAND FIRM, KEEP YOUR RESOLVE

The only best-answers for keeping your resolve are the ones that work for you, that keep the relationships you want to maintain in place, and that allow you to live your life to your greatest sense of accomplishment, achievement, and well-being.

1. Go back over the list of Fifty Mantras and circle three or four strategies that you'll use in the next three months to say *no*, mean *no*, and stick to it.

2. The next time you say *no*, how will you stand firm and keep your resolve?

3. The next time you find your *no* turning into a *yes*, how will you keep your *no* response in place?

4. What mantra or strategy would you add to the above list? (Feel free to share it with us by using the form in Appendix E.)

## POWER PRACTICE: SEE YOURSELF AS A MASTER OF NO

Draw a picture of yourself as a Master of No. Include how you feel, who is around you, where you are, and how you are holding your body and your head to communicate your *no*. Also include an image of what happens after you've said *no* out loud.

## THE BOTTOM LINE

Stop thinking that *no* means *maybe*, that *maybe* means *yes* and that *yes* means *no*. Start right now using the words *no* to mean *no*, *maybe* to mean that it could go either way, and *yes* to mean *yes*. *Yes* can convert to *no* if the terms change or promises aren't kept. *No* might convert to a *yes* when the terms, options, timelines, and rights are redefined in ways that allow you to say *yes*. The key is to apply the Power of No Model so that you can be decisive, stop waffling, and say *no* when you need to.

Stop waffling. Start making clear decisions. Keep your resolve. "Exercise the power of saying *no* to anything that compromises your authentic self," said an unknown author. Give up feeling obligated to say *yes* to everything. Claim this attitude: "There is a time for *yes*, a time for *no* and a time for *maybe*. I know the difference. I will stand firm in my use of yes, *no* and maybe."

As a Master of No, see yourself as:

1. A confident decision maker.

2. A competent decision maker.

3. A bridge to help build understanding so that best-decisions can get made.

4. Someone who uses *no* as an ethical response that serves the highest good of all concerned.

## POWER CLOSE

1. Apply the Power of No Model to gather information.

2. Make the best possible decision you can make with the information you have.

3. Don't waffle! Waffles are great to eat, and horrible for decision making.

4. State your decision clearly.

5. Own it.

6. Keep your resolve.

7. Work with whatever happens.

8. Don't beat yourself up or be too hard on yourself when things don't go as planned or expected.

9. Keep moving forward.

# Acknowledgments

I am very appreciative of all the people who have contributed to the successful completion of this book. "Thank you" merely begins to convey my gratitude.

## THE ORIGINAL JUMP-STARTERS

- Tom Brown, who said, "You should write a book on 1,001 ways to say no."
- A woman in Maryland whose inability to say *no* inspired me to say "No. It is an important, valuable, and viable word, and more people need it in their vocabulary."
- Meeting & Management Essentials' time management workshop attendees who discussed, brainstormed about, and debated the best ways to say *no*.
- My sister, Mary Murray, who knew this project was in the works when during a cocktail party conversation she discovered author Sarah Fister Gale, who had worked with book broker Stan Wakefield. The short story is that Stan put me in contact with AMACOM executive editor Jacqueline Flynn. Jacquie's expert editing helped me to improve my skills and to refine the book that is here in your hands.

## MAJOR CONTENT CONTRIBUTORS

*David W. Gill*

David W. Gill, Ph.D., is an ethics writer and consultant based in Berkeley, California. He is a regular columnist ("Benchmark Ethics") for *Ethix* magazine published by the Institute for Business, Technology, and Ethics (*www.ethix.org*), which he co-founded in 1998. His current research focuses on how to measure the ethical health of organizations, how to implement ethics and values statements in organizational structures and daily practices, and how to find common ethical standards in a diverse, global business environment. Gill is the author of six books, including *Becoming Good: Building Moral Character* (InterVarsity Press, 2000) and *Doing Right: Practicing Ethical Principles* (InterVarsity Press, in press).

## Chris Kent

Internationally recognized as a teacher, educator, professional consultant, and author, Chris Kent is one of the world's foremost authorities on *Jeet Kune Do*, the revolutionary martial arts and self-help philosophy developed by the legendary Bruce Lee. An active instructor and business owner, as well as a prolific writer, Chris has written four books and created two instructional videotape series on the martial art of *Jeet Kune Do*. Chris is a frequent contributing writer to numerous national and international martial arts publications. His articles have been published in over eight languages and have appeared in every major martial arts publication in the world, including *Inside Kung Fu*, *Black Belt*, *Martial Arts Illustrated*, and *Budo International*.

## Dave Lakhani

Dave Lakhani, president of Bold Approach, Inc. and a multipreneur, is responsible for developing dynamic strategies that have driven record-breaking growth and increases in sales in more than 500 businesses in the past ten years. Dave is an in-demand speaker, author, and trainer, whose ideas have been applied by some of the biggest companies in the United States. His latest book, *Bold Approach Business*, is a classic text on rapid growth tactics for businesses that need more revenue and profitable sales today. Dave is frequently seen in magazines including *Selling Power*, *Sales and Marketing Management*, *Entrepreneur*, *Business Solutions*, *Retail Systems Reseller*, *Integrated Solutions*, *Home Office Computing*, *PC Magazine*, and in other media including *Business Radio Network*, *The Business Connection*, *The Today Show*, and dozens more.

## Robert Spencer

Robert Spencer is recognized internationally as a teacher of the Feldenkrais Method. He is a renegade psychotherapist, Master Practitioner of

Neuro-Linguistic Programming, author of the book *The Craft of the Warrior*, founder of Idaho's Sendero Institute of Consciousness Studies, and guide to many areas of human potential. Since 1984 he has taught Feldenkrais classes to the general public, actors, athletes, equestrians, and chronic pain sufferers. His lively and informative style guarantees that the effects of his teaching will remain with his audiences long after the class is over.

## CONTRIBUTORS OF STORIES OF *NO*

Linda Alden, communications manager, Boise (formerly Boise Cascade)

Sharon Ashcraft, The Arc, Inc.

Alita Ashmore, physical therapist

Christopher Avery, author of *Teamwork Is an Individual Skill*, and international authority on productive work relationships. *www.partnerwerks.com*

John Bernardo, corporate manager of resource conservation for Albertsons, Inc.

The Honorable Gregory S. Casey, president and CEO, BIPAC in Washington, D.C., and partner in Veritas Advisors, LLP in Boise, Idaho

Brad Cleveland, president and CEO, Incoming Calls Management Institute, Annapolis, Maryland. *www.incoming.com*

Patti Danos, publicist, Chicago, Illinois

Tom Drews, speaker and founder of What Works! Communications

Shirlene Elledge, Adlerian Relationship Center

Brenda Fake, principal consultant, EMA Services

Annie Berry Gigray, retired personnel/communications specialist, Hewlett-Packard

Connie Goldstein, magazine editor, Sarasota, Florida

Deni Hoehne, human resources executive, CRI Advantage

Vickie Schaffeld Holbrook, managing editor, *Idaho Press-Tribune*

Sylvia Hunt, Caldwell Fine Arts director and organ teacher

Jim Kemp, retired extension agent and active community volunteer

Lisa Leff, vice president and portfolio manager

Marguerite Mason, former corporate executive, business owner and business development consultant

Colleen Maile, writer, editor, mother

Cindy Peterson, 1976 Olympian, mother, and working professional

Iris Sasaki, Portland, Oregon

Judy Sullivan, *in memoriam*: friend, sister, wife, mother
Trish Terranova, Seattle, Washington
Richard Tremblay, business management consultant, Idaho

## ADDITIONAL SUPPORT

Rob Beltramo, confidential business consultant, who provided hours of research.
Rinda Just and Pam Graham, who volunteered to be manuscript readers.
Angie Krommenhoek, who provided artwork.
Julie Griffin Levitt, best-selling author, trainer and presenter, who read Chapter 1 when it was still in very rough form.
Steven Piersanti and Ed Gordon, who read and made suggestions on early versions of the proposal for this book.
And Al Patz, Lois Kemp, and all of you who cheered the writing process on.

# The Power of No Self-Assessment and Advanced Power Practices

To discover what your typical ability to say *no* is, respond to the following self-assessment to discover whether you are a:

Master of No (you can say *no* effectively now)
Waffler (you mostly say *maybe*)
Yes-ism person (you usually say *yes*)

And to discover what messages you tend to rely on: *no*, never, mostly *maybe*, or usually *yes*.

The following self-assessment is for information and learning purposes. The self-assessment, which is not a validated assessment or test and therefore not predictive, gives you an idea of whether you tend to say *no*, *maybe*, or *yes* most of the time. It is not meant to be reproduced and is meant to be used in place in this book.

# THE POWER OF NO SELF-ASSESSMENT

*Responding Directions*

1. Picture yourself in any of the situations in which you have actually said *no* or have had an opportunity to say *no*.

2. As you read each of the twenty-one statements or questions, consider whether you often say these very words or something similar. If you say them often, put a mark in the Strongly Agree box. If you don't say the words often or at all, put a mark in the Strongly Disagree box. And if you neither strongly agree nor strongly disagree, consider which "Mildly" statement best fits. Be sure you end up with just twenty-one marks.

| I often find myself saying something similar to: | Strongly Agree | Mildly Agree | Mildly Disagree | Strongly Disagree |
|---|---|---|---|---|
| 1. No. | | | | |
| 2. Couldn't you find someone else? | | | | |
| 3. My schedule is full right now, try me in a few months. | | | | |
| 4. I could do that if you can't find anyone else. | | | | |
| 5. My schedule doesn't allow me to take that on right now. | | | | |
| 6. No way. | | | | |
| 7. No, thank you. | | | | |
| 8. I'm sorry I can't help out. | | | | |
| 9. I'm willing to serve. | | | | |
| 10. What part of *no* don't you understand? | | | | |
| 11. I don't think I'm the best person for this. | | | | |

| | | | | |
|---|---|---|---|---|
| 12. I could probably help out. | | | | |
| 13. My schedule doesn't allow me to take that on at all. | | | | |
| 14. Maybe later. | | | | |
| 15. I'd be happy to. | | | | |
| 16. I won't do that at all. | | | | |
| 17. Maybe. | | | | |
| 18. How can I help? | | | | |
| 19. Stop. Don't do that. | | | | |
| 20. I think I've already taken on too much. | | | | |
| 21. Yes. | | | | |

### Scoring Directions

1. For each of the twenty-one items, transfer your responses by circling the number in the corresponding level of agreement column on the scoring grid that follows.

2. After you have circled twenty-one numbers (one for each item), add the numbers together for a grand total.

3. Locate your grand total in the Power of No Self-assessment Results Grid and learn how well you really say *no*.

4. Then read the section titled "What the Self-Assessment Tells Us" in Chapter 1 to learn more about yourself and others.

### Scoring The Power of No Self-Assessment

| I often find myself saying something similar to: | Strongly Agree | Mildly Agree | Mildly Disagree | Strongly Disagree |
|---|---|---|---|---|
| **Sample**   1. No. | 4 | 3 | 2 | [1] |
| 1. No. | 4 | 3 | 2 | 1 |
| 2. Couldn't you find someone else? | 1 | 2 | 3 | 3 |

| | | | | |
|---|---|---|---|---|
| 3. My schedule is full right now, try me in a few months. | 1 | 2 | 3 | 3 |
| 4. I could do that if you can't find anyone else. | 1 | 2 | 3 | 3 |
| 5. My schedule doesn't allow me to take that on right now. | 2 | 2 | 1 | 1 |
| 6. No way. | 4 | 3 | 2 | 1 |
| 7. No, thank you. | 4 | 3 | 2 | 1 |
| 8. I'm sorry I can't help out. | 2 | 2 | 3 | 3 |
| 9. I'm willing to serve. | 1 | 2 | 3 | 3 |
| 10. What part of *no* don't you understand? | 3 | 3 | 2 | 1 |
| 11. I don't think I'm the best person for this. | 3 | 2 | 2 | 2 |
| 12. I could probably help out. | 1 | 2 | 3 | 4 |
| 13. My schedule doesn't allow me to take that on at all. | 4 | 3 | 2 | 1 |
| 14. Maybe later. | 1 | 2 | 3 | 3 |
| 15. I'd be happy to. | 1 | 2 | 3 | 4 |
| 16. I won't do that at all. | 4 | 3 | 2 | 1 |
| 17. Maybe. | 1 | 1 | 3 | 3 |
| 18. How can I help? | 1 | 2 | 3 | 4 |
| 19. Stop. Don't do that. | 4 | 3 | 2 | 1 |
| 20. I think I've already taken on too much. | 1 | 1 | 3 | 3 |
| 21. Yes. | 1 | 2 | 3 | 4 |

**Power of No Grand Total** _____

## Results Grid

| If your point total is: | When it comes to saying no, you are a: |
|---|---|
| 63–77 | *Master of No*: a person who can say *no* graciously and effectively whenever you choose. |
| 42–62 | *Waffler*: a person who can't say *no* and can't say *yes* clearly so mostly says *maybe*. |
| 23–41 | *Yes-ism person*: a person who usually says *yes*. |

## ADVANCED POWER PRACTICES

The original Power of No Model is:

**P**urpose
**O**ptions/Resources available
**W**hen/Timing
**E**motional ties
**R**ights and Responsibilities.

*POWER Model 2*

Still more questions can be posed in the process of determining whether to say *yes* or *no*. For instance, the POWER Model 2 includes these arenas of questions.

**P**riority *Decision-Making.* Use the Priority Decision Grid found in Chapter 3.

**O**bligation. Determine what is already obligated. Determine what will be obligated if you say *yes* and if you say *no.*

**W**hy, *Who, and When.* Establish why the request is being made and when the deadline is. Also establish who will be available to help you get things done.

**E**nergy *required.* Assess how much of your energy will be required to complete the request.

**R**eason *and Results.* Determine the reason for the request and ask for a description of the expected results.

## POWER PRACTICE: POWER MODEL 2

1.  When would these question arenas be more helpful to you than the original Power of No Model arenas?

2.  Who else in your company will you enlist to begin using the Power of No Models for decision making?

3.  What will you do to commit to memory the five key questions of the original Power of No Model?

## POWER Model 3

Here is one more approach to the arena of questions that can be posed in the process of determining whether to say *yes* or *no*. The POWER Model 3 includes these arenas of questions.

**P**eople. Who needs to be involved to complete the task?
**O**pportunity. Is there a realistic opportunity to complete the task?
**W**hat. What exactly needs to be done?
**E**xchange. What's the trade? What will you give up? What will you gain?
**R**esources Required. What is required to complete the task in the agreed upon manner?

## POWER PRACTICE: POWER MODEL 3

1.  When would these question arenas be more helpful to you than the original Power of No Model arenas or the POWER Model 2 questions?

2.  Who in your community, family, or social life can support your improved decision making?

3.  What will you do to continue refining your ability to apply the Power of No Model in daily conversations?

## POWER PRACTICE: COUNTER INDECISION

### Scenario 1. Business Meeting Indecision

You are not the meeting leader. A decision is needed in the meeting today, or the company will miss an important opportunity and bid-submission deadline. Your expertise is needed to help make the decision of whether to bid or not-bid. Ten people are in the room. Some are talking in circles, some are staring into space, some are resisting the ideas being discussed, and some of you are so frustrated that you are ready to do something. It's time for a decision to be made.

What will you say?
What part of the Power of No Model will you use with this group?
What will you ask of the meeting members?
What tone of voice and body language will you use?

## Scenario 2. Home-Front Decision Challenges

Your family is waiting on your final decision to start making plans for this year's summer vacation. You promised to do some research that you haven't gotten to yet. Work has been crazy and you haven't even been thinking about a vacation. Your kids are bothering you for a decision nearly every day.

> What will you say?
> What will you ask to collect enough information to make a decision?
> What tone of voice and body language will you use?

## Scenario 3. Community Decision Challenges

You are at the annual meeting of the neighborhood association for the subdivision you live in. About fifty people are present. The Board is not leading the meeting with clarity or control. A motion has been made and the Board president doesn't seem to have heard it. Members are starting several side-conversations. The Waffler in you wants to leave. The struggling master of No that you've newly found for yourself is ready to offer to help move the meeting forward.

> What will you say?
> What questions could you ask?
> What tone of voice and body language will you use?

# *Long List*

Ways to Say *No*

The words used to say *no* are as varied as we are. The key to success in being clearly understood is to use the word *no* in your response so that the listener has a better chance of hearing your *no*. The words, phrases, sentences, and questions that follow are workshop attendees, friends, family members, clients, coworkers, and volunteers speaking or writing the ways they say *no*. You'll likely find words that you use to say *no*. You'll see some you won't use because they don't fit your style, might get you fired, or might destroy a relationship. Some words and phrases you'll see on the *no-never* list and on the *no-maybe* list because the tone of voice and body language used to deliver the words can change your meaning.

You'll also likely spot words that you'd like to use in the future. Highlight the words and phrases that work for you. Also add your own tried and true phrases. Then, every time you discover you have not said *no* when you wanted or needed to, come back to this list and practice with renewed energy and focus on saying *no*.

## WORDS TO SAY *NO*

The phrases that follow, once used, have to be followed by your sticking to your word. Otherwise, you negate the word *no* all over again and move immediately to being a Waffler. Revisit Chapter 10, Keep Your Resolve, for stick-to-it strategies.

No.
No!

No!!

No, thank you.

No, not now.

No, not ever.

No, I can't fit it in.

"N" "O"

Read my lips, No.

What part of *no* don't you understand?

NO (shouted).

No (firmly).

No (confidently).

No (like you mean *no* from the depth of your being).

No means *no*.

No, that's bad.

No, they're bad for you. You don't want to eat that.

Not happening.

I understand your need, my plate is full currently. Here's my
    suggestion on who can assist you . . .

No way.

No, I don't need your help.

Absolutely not.

By no means can that be done.

Negative.

The answer is in the negative.

Nix.

Nyet (Russian).

Nein (German).

No (Spanish).

Non (French).

Rejected.

Annulled.

NO. Get away from me.

No. Don't touch me.

No. Step back now.

No. Leave right now.

No. Don't come near me.

No, don't let your dog near me.

No, don't let your cat near me.

No. Just look.

No. Don't get in, it's too hot.

No. Stand back.

No running.

No swimming.
No diving.
No fishing.
No trespassing.
No hunting.
No dumping.
No soliciting.
No smoking.
No shirt, no shoes, no service.
No, I don't have the authority.
No, I don't have time for that project.
No, I don't have time to do this for you.
We are not able to handle that line of business in our department.
I'm not the appropriate person to do this. _____ is the right
      person to contact, and his/her number is _____.
I can't do that for you.
I can't correct your bill. You'll have to talk to _____.

Depending on the potential of actually obtaining the resources listed
below, these statements could be a *no,* or a *maybe.*

We don't have the time to do it.
We don't have the staff to do it.
We don't have the budget to do it.
We don't have the facility to do it.
We don't have the equipment to do it.
We don't have people trained to do it.
No money.
No budget.
No cash flow.
No authority.
No staff time is available.
No allocated resources.
No time.
No. My schedule is full.
No my plate is full.
No. Thanks for thinking of me.
No, please take me off your list.
Not willing to do that.
Not going to do that.
No. I'll assign it to _____.
No I'll delegate it to _____.

This is a waste of time. I'm not doing it.

Sorry, no, I can't go with you.

Sorry, no, I can't go with you, I'm doing _____ today.

Won't do it.

No contact.

Do not mail.

Do not call.

Do not leave a message.

Do not _____.

No, I won't.

No, I wouldn't.

No, I didn't.

No, I haven't (and so on, with He, She, We, They).

I disown that.

No, that's not okay.

Not on your life.

No can do.

Not in a million years.

I veto that.

I nix that idea.

Thumbs down (spoken or hands used to signal this).

That's forbidden.

I forbid that.

That's against the rules.

That's against the policies.

Prohibited.

That's prohibited.

That plan was rejected.

That plan was voted down.

The vote failed.

We didn't reach agreement.

We didn't have a quorum.

We didn't take a legal vote.

We didn't achieve consensus.

The request has been denied.

The order was cancelled.

The request was turned down.

Disallowed.

That behavior is not acceptable.

No, don't do that.

Don't do it. That's taboo.

Stop.

Stop it.

Stop it right now.
It's none of your business. I won't discuss it.

***Your Favorite Ways to Say* No**

## Saying *No* for Others or at Work

No, she's not available for that project.
No, he doesn't have the skills you need.
No, that team isn't free.
No, I can't free up that team (or person). They are already assigned.
We outlawed that.
Denied.
Refused.
I refuse.
Dismissed.
Nothing further.
End of discussion.
Overruled.
That option was thrown out of consideration.
That option was eliminated.
Abandon the plan.
Abort.
Scrap that now.
Scratch that.
Withdrawn.
No more.
No, I don't know the answer.
No, we can't take on any new projects.

***Your Favorite Ways to Say* No *on Behalf of Others or at Work***

## Social and Family Situations

No, that's not in your best interest.
No, that's not in our best interest.

No, I'm not up for a movie.
No, that's not good for you.
No, he can't go to the dance.
No, she can't stay out past 10 P.M.
No, I'm too tired.
No, I'm not at my best.
No, we don't need that.
No, we won't have the money for that.
No, I won't buy that for you.
No, put it back.
No. Don't touch.
No teasing.
No hitting.
No punching.
No throwing the ball in the house.
No. You need to go to bed now.
Enough already. I said no.
No, I don't drink alcohol.
No, I don't do drugs.
No, I don't smoke.
No, I don't have sex.
No, I don't have unprotected sex.
No, No (as spoken to a child).
No (as defiantly spoken by your two-year old).
No (as defiantly spoken by your thirteen-year old).
No (as stated by your nearly-legal-age child).
Not really (as answer to "don't you want any?").
No more.

### *Your Favorite Ways to Say* No *in Family or Friendship Situations*

## WAFFLER WORDS AND PHRASES

*No, maybe.* These Waffler phrases leave you on the line to still end up having to do something. When you use these phrase you are putting off a decision, potentially misleading someone into thinking you've said *yes,* and you may find yourself doing something you didn't want to do. So, beware. When you find yourself using any of the word on this list, an alarm should go off in your mind. And the alarm message is, "Get out the Power of No Model decision-tools as quickly as possible. Stop waffling and make a decision."

Maybe.
Maybe?
Maybe!
No?
No, not now maybe later.
Not now maybe later.
No, let's reschedule.
Is it important enough that I should drop everything else?
I would like to but my other priority is to get task _____ or project _____ done.
I can't fit it in.
I can't fit it into my schedule right now. Check back with me.
I can't complete this within your timeframe.
I'm sorry. I just can't at this time.
I don't have time.
I don't have time right now.
I don't want to.
No time—too many other things to do.
I have other things that have to be done first.
My schedule is booked.
My schedule has no openings.
Is there someone else available to do it?
Someone else with better expertise in this area could do it.
Someone else with better expertise in this area should do it.
I'm not the right person. Maybe _____ could do it.
I don't have the right skills. Maybe _____ could do it.
I'm not the right person for that. _____ really likes to do that.
Is there anyone else who can get this for you?
I'm bogged down right now. Can this wait?
Can it wait?
Can't it wait?
Do you have to have that now?
This is my priority list. You let me know what the priorities are for me to work on.
Here's my project load. What would you have me drop to take on this project?

Which project is most important to you?

I'm working on other high priority projects at this time and do not
　　have time.

"Failure to plan on your part does not constitute crisis on my part."
　　(Original source unknown.)

You wanted it when?

No, I don't have the resources.

Not interested.

Don't want to.

Not able to do that.

I don't know how to do that.

No, we don't have the money for that.

Please place your request right here (tactfully said while pointing at
　　your in-box).

We do not have the required information to provide a quote.

Would it be okay if I recommended someone else?

Would it be okay if I delegated this?

I can do this if I don't do ＿＿＿＿＿＿＿. Which one is more
　　important?

Send me an e-mail with what is needed and when.

If you want me to do this, I will need ＿＿＿＿＿＿
　　and ＿＿＿＿＿＿ first.

This will put me into overtime.

You didn't have an appointment.

I'm not making a decision today.

I don't have the budget now.

Ignore that.

We'll see.

Withdrawn.

(Ignore the question or request completely.)

It depends.

It depends, what's up?

It depends on what you want done.

It depends on when you need it to be done.

It depends on what you want me to drop off of my to-do list.

It depends on who else is available to help get this done.

**_Your Favorite Ways to Say_ No**

## *Yes, Later. No, Not Now, Definitely Later*

Beware of these. An overuse of these will put you right back in the Yes-ism person spot that you are reading this book to overcome. (That's also why this list is so short.)

> I can't do it at this time but I will be available in two weeks.
> I'd like to help you, I could do that in eight weeks.
> I can get to that _____ (give a day, date and time).
> I see that you have a problem that needs attention now. How can I
>     help you?

### *Your Favorite Ways to Say No, Not Now, but I Will Later*

Of course there are millions of variations. For more ideas on saying no, see Appendix D.

# Resources and Further Readings

## ASSERTIVENESS-RELATED TITLES

Axelrod, Alan and Jim Holtje, *201 Ways to Say No Gracefully and Effectively* (New York: McGraw-Hill, 1997).

Braiker, Harriet B., *The Disease to Please* (New York: McGraw-Hill, 2001).

Breitman, Patti and Connie Hatch, *How to SAY NO Without Feeling Guilty* (New York: Broadway Books, 2000).

Cloud, Henry and John Townsend, *Boundaries: When to Say YES, When to Say NO to Take Control of Your Life* (Grand Rapids, Mich.: Zondervan Publishing, 1992).

Fensterheim, Herbert and Jean Baer, *Don't Say Yes When You Want to Say No* (New York: Dell Publishing, 1975).

Johnson, Spencer, M.D., *"Yes" or "No": The Guide to Better Decisions* (New York: HarperCollins, 1992).

Robinson, Duke, *Too Nice for Your Own Good* (New York: Warner Books, 1997).

Smith, Manuel J., *When I Say No, I Feel Guilty* (New York: Bantam Books, 1975).

## COMMUNICATION SKILLS READINGS

Adler, Mortimer J., *How to Speak, How to Listen* (New York: Collier Books, 1983).

Brennan, Charles D. Jr., *Sales Questions That Close the Sale.* (New York: AMACOM, 1994).

DeBecker, Gavin, *The Gift of Fear* (Boston: Little, Brown, 1997).

Deep, Sam and Lyle Sussman, *What to Ask When You Don't Know What to Say* (Englewood Cliffs, N.J.: Prentice Hall, 1993).

Fisher, Roger and William Ury, *Getting to Yes* (New York: Penguin Books, 1981).

Harkins, Phil, *Powerful Conversations* (New York: McGraw-Hill, 1999).

Kolbell, Erik, *LifeScripts for Family & Friends* (New York: Pocket Books, 2002).

Leeds, Dorothy, *SmartQuestions* (New York: Berkley Books, 1987).

———, *PowerSpeak* (New York: Berkley Books, 1988).

———, *The 7 Powers of Questions* (New York: Perigee Book, Berkley Publishing, 2000).

Lustberg, Arch, *How to Sell Yourself* (Franklin Lakes, N.J.: Career Press, 2002).

Miller, John G., *QBQ!—The Question Behind the Question.* Denver, Colo.: Denver Press, 2001).

Peterson, Walt, *5000 Ways to Say No to Your Children* (Fort Bragg, Calif.: Mendocino Coast Press, 1993).

Pollan, Stephen M. and Mark Levine, *LifeScripts* (New York: John Wiley, 1996).

# Share Your Story: Get a Book

How do *you* say *no*? This book is the 101 Course on saying *no*. There are millions of ways to say *no* and hundreds of ways to keep your resolve. Are you willing to share your story of how you say *no*? If so, and if it is used in a future book, I'll send you a copy. Please share your stories of saying *no*.

1. Share a story of when you said *no* and it worked.

2. Share a story of when you said *no* and it didn't work.

3. Share the actual words you use when you say *no* to people at work.

4. Share the actual words you use when you say *no* to people at home.

5. Feel free to share any *no* story that you have or have heard.

6. How do you keep your resolve once you've said *no*?
   Many thanks. And here's to your say-no success!

*Send your stories by mail, Web site, or e-mail to:*
Meeting & Management Essentials
P.O. Box 8045
Boise, Idaho 83707
*www.stopwaffling.com*
*jana@janakemp.com*

# Index

assets, protection of, 48–49
attitude, in self-defense, 41
awareness, in self-defense, 41

choices, in daily living, 122–123
consequences
　of choice, 191
　of saying *no,* 65–68
　of saying *yes,* 139
　of waffling, 115–116

decision making, 34–36
　business scenario, 207
　community scenarios, 156–158, 208
　creating time and space for,
　　104–105
　in daily life, 143–144
　in family situations, 156
　finding right balance in, 72
　having a choice, 122–123
　home-front scenarios, 151–153, 208
　Power of No Model used in, 148–
　　158, 166
　and Priority Decision Grid, 39–40
　standing firm, 190
　in work situations, 149–151
detailed say-no personality, 90, 96–98
direct say-no personality, 90, 96–98

emotional space, protection of, 50–51
emotional ties
　as Power of No Model decision
　　point, 26–27, 29

sample questions, 33–34
and saying *yes,* 135
and waffling, 120
emotions
　recognition of, 26–27
　in response to requests, 26

Fischer, Paul, 62
flakey-waffler consequences, 115
force, use of
　communication as, 48
　deadly, 48
　personal presence as, 47
　physical techniques as, 48
freedom, and the power of *no,* 61–63

Gandhi, Mahatma, 62
Gill, David W., 61–62, 107, 191,
　　197–198
gracious say-no personality, 90, 96–98
greedy say-no personality, 91, 96–98

Hanks, Tom, 62
health, protection of, 59
Holbrook, Vickie, 28

indirect say-no personality, 90, 96–98
inspired say-no personality, 91, 96–98
integrity, protection of, 53–54
intellectual space, protection of, 49–50

Jeet Kune Do, 41
John Paul II, Pope, 193

Kent, Chris, 41, 45–46, 191, 198

Lakhani, Dave, 177, 198
legitimate-waffler consequences,
    115–116

martial arts, *see* self-defense
Mason, Marguerite, 138
Master of No, *see also no;* saying *no*
    characteristics of, 195
    defined, 8
    ethical behavior, 78
    knowing when to say *yes,* 138–139
    say-no approach, 13, 15
    say-no personalities, 91–94
*maybe*
    *see also* saying *maybe;* Wafflers; waf-
        fling
    statements, 116–117
    turned into *no,* 117–118, 124–126
    turned into *yes,* 128, 129
mental space, protection of, 49–50

*no, see also* saying *no*
    as an act of freedom, 61–63
    creating clear messages, 86–87
    defined, 3
    internal/external mismatch, 80–82
    owning the word, 190
    and self-defense, 41
    setting boundaries with, 190
    turned into *yes,* 146–147
    underestimating power of, 192
    used in signs, 88
    used with children, 3
    used with family and friends, 89

options
    as Power of No Model decision
        point, 23–24, 29
    in responding to requests, 23–24
    sample questions, 31–32
    and saying *yes,* 135
    and waffling, 119–120

personal space
    cultural attitudes about, 51
    protection of, 51–53

"please say yes" tactics, 6
Policy of No statements, 75–77, 106–
    107, 162–165
Power of No Consequences, 66–67
    effect on decision making, 158–161
    say-no statements, 69–72
Power of No Model, 20
    applied to practice scenarios,
        177–182
    decision making, 34–36, 143–144
        in community situation, 138
        in community situations,
            156–158
        in family situations, 151–153, 156
        in work situations, 149–151
    decision points, 21–27
    emotional *vs.* logical elements, 29
    and ethics, 74–75, 77–78
    Model 2, 206
    Model 3, 207
    questions, 85
Power of No Self-Assessment, 8
    questionnaire, 9–10, 202–205
    scoring chart, 11–12, 205
preparation, in self-defense, 41
Priority Decision Grid, 39, 193
protection
    of your assets, 48–49
    of your health, 59–57
    of your integrity, 53–54
    of your money, 58–59
    of your personal space, 49–53
    of your spiritual well-being, 54–56
    of your time, 56–57
purpose
    and personal priorities, 23
    as Power of No Model decision
        point, 21–22, 29
    of requests, 21–22
    sample questions, 30–31
    and saying *yes,* 135
    and waffling, 119

Quick Tip Guides, 185–187

requests
    confirming legality, 27

confirming reasonableness of, 27
emotions in response to, 26
identifying deadlines, 24–25
options in response to, 24–25
Power of No Model used with, 30
resources in response to, 23–24
setting boundaries, 28
understanding the purpose, 21–22
resources
    as Power of No Model decision
        point, 29
    in responding to requests, 23–24
    sample questions, 31–32
    and saying *yes,* 135
    and waffling, 119–120
responsibilities
    and personal expectations, 28
    as Power of No Model decision
        point, 27–28, 29
    sample questions, 34
    and saying *yes,* 135–136
    and waffling, 120
rights
    and personal expectations, 28
    as Power of No Model decision
        point, 27, 29
    sample questions, 34
    and saying *yes,* 135–136
    and waffling, 120

saying *maybe, see also maybe*
    quick tips for, 186
    sample phrases, 215–216
    the Wafflers' style, 13–14
saying *no, see also no*
    to bad debts, 58
    based on personality, 89–91
    body language tools for, 46
    to children *vs.* adults, 192
    consequences of, 65–66, 191
    counting the times of, 148
    difficulty of, 5–6
    effect on decision making, 158–161
    ethical basis for, 61–64
    ethical strategy for, 74–75
    finding the words for, 144
    as form of respect, 192

to friends and family, 6
graciously, 102–104
at home *vs.* work, 4
the Master of No's style, 13
*not now*
    sample phrases, 217
    the Waffler's style, 13–14
    the Yes-ism person's style, 14
for now, *yes* later, 131
out loud, 84–85, 147–148, 192
practicing, 86
protecting yourself while, 36, 38–39
as protection of your
    assets, 48–49
    health, 59–57
    integrity, 53–54
    money, 58–59
    personal space, 49–53
    spiritual well-being, 54–56
    time, 56–57
quick tips for, 185
responsibility for, 63–64
sample phrases, 209–214
with say-no personalities, 97–98
scenarios, 167–177
in social and family settings,
    213–214
strategies for, 74–75, 189–193
three styles, 13–14
and tone of voice, 46–47
various ways of, 4
visualizing, 83, 85
when it doesn't work, 107–108
words used for, 87–88, 105–106
in the workplace, 7, 213
in writing, 191
saying *yes, see also yes;* Yes-ism persons
    consequences of, 139
    dilemmas of, 5
    internal/external mismatch,
        132–134
    out loud, 136
    and Power of No Model, 134–136
    quick tips for, 186–187
    by remaining silent, 4
    in response to "please," 6

say-no approaches
of Masters of No, 13–15
messages in, 18
recognition of, 17–18
skill levels, 15–17
of Wafflers, 15–16
of Yes-ism persons, 16
say-no personalities, 90–91
identification of, 98–102
perceptions about, 96
saying *no* with, 97–98
say-no presence, 90–91
self-defense, 41–42, *see also* force, use
of
and body language, 45–46
effective stance for, 41–42
importance of stance, 44
police lessons, 47–48
on the street, 45
self-protection, *see* protection; self-
defense
self-talk, 82–83
signs
*no* used in, 88
waffler, 126–127
slavery, moral question of, 62–63
Spencer, Robert, 198–199
spiritual well-being, protection of,
54–55

time
better uses of, 57
protection of, 56–57

Wafflers
defined, 8
flakey, 113–115

integrity, 53
legitimate, 113–115
say-no approach, 13–14, 15–16
say-no personality, 91
types, 113–114
waffler signs, 126–127
waffling, *see also maybe;* saying *maybe*
consequences of, 115–116
defined, 111
examples, 112
flakey, 113–115
legitimate, 113–115, 186
and Power of No Model, 119–121
reasons for, 112
and teenagers, 123
types, 113–114
when is it okay?, 121–123
when
as Power of No Model decision
point, 24–25, 29
sample questions, 32–33
and saying *yes,* 135
and waffling, 120
women's right to vote, 63
workplace, pressure to say *yes,* 7

*yes, see also* saying *yes*
ethics, 140
power, 5
statements, 140–141
yes-economy, 58
Yes-ism persons
defined, 8
ethical behavior, 78
integrity, 54
say-no approach, 14, 16
say-no personality, 91

# About the Author

Jana M. Kemp is the founder and owner of Meeting & Management Essentials, which focuses on improving decision-making, meeting, and time management skills for individuals and organizations. Jana's business approaches include aerobic listening, knowledge brokering, time architecting, strategic question-asking, and decision-prompting that inspires action.

Jana has brought the power of productivity, morale, and profit to day-to-day business meetings and operations since 1986. She is the author of *Moving Meetings* (McGraw Hill, English version in 1994, and released in Italian in 1999) and the publisher of the quarterly online newsletter *Better Meetings for Everyone*. Jana has also served as a business columnist for the *Idaho Press-Tribune* and *Idaho Business Review* newspapers, as a business segment provider for television news networks, and as a business radio show host for four years. Her time management expertise was tapped for content editing of the *Unofficial Guide to Managing Time* by Dawn Reno (IDG Books Worldwide, Inc., 2000).

In 2004, Jana chose to test her skills and to serve the state of Idaho by successfully running for the Idaho House of Representatives. All of her facilitation, moderation, catalytic question asking, and clear decision-making skills are put to good use in public service.

Jana's clients include a variety of organizations such as: Fortune 100 companies, nonprofits, associations, conference-holders, and government agencies. For more information about Jana Kemp and her availability to speak for your organization, conference, or corporation, visit *www.jana kemp.com* and *www.StopWaffling.com*, email jana@janakemp.com, or call 800-701-9447.